Managing Sticky
Situations at Work

Managing Sticky Situations at Work

Communication Secrets for Success in the Workplace

Joan C. Curtis

Praeger

An Imprint of ABC-CLIO, LLC

A B C **CLIO**

Santa Barbara, California • Denver, Colorado • Oxford, England

Library of Congress Cataloging-in-Publication Data

Curtis, Joan C., 1950– Managing sticky situations at work : communication secrets for
    success in the workplace / Joan C. Curtis.
      p. cm.
    Includes bibliographical references and index.
    ISBN 978-0-313-36278-1 (hard copy : alk. paper) — ISBN 978-0-313-36279-8 (ebook)
1. Communication in management. I. Title.
HD30.3.C86   2009
658.4'5—dc22   2009011685

13 12 11 10 9   1 2 3 4 5

This book is also available on the World Wide Web as an eBook.
Visit www.abc-clio.com for details.

ABC-CLIO, LLC
130 Cremona Drive, P.O. Box 1911
Santa Barbara, California 93116-1911

This book is printed on acid-free paper ∞

Manufactured in the United States of America

Contents

Illustrations

Acknowledgments

As a disclaimer, all the people described in this book are loosely based on real-life incidents. None of them represent actual people I know. I thank all those individuals, however, who shared "sticky situation" examples that I could draw on for this book. If you recognize friends, co-workers, bosses, or clients, it is purely coincidental.

My special thanks go to my husband who diligently read each chapter and added his unique comments. As a psychiatrist, his particular vision and knowledge provided a unique insight I found truly valuable. I also thank my coaching colleagues and clients who shared situations from which I loosely drew examples and, sometimes, limericks (thank you, Joanne).

Introduction: How to Say It Just Right in the Workplace

A colleague asks you to recommend him for a promotion. You know he is less than adequate. In fact, you've had to complete his work to make deadlines. What do you do?

You supervise a group of six professionals. You were promoted from within their ranks. Each has worked at the job longer than you, but you have more formal education. The group is now sabotaging your every move. What do you do?

Your boss blocks you from making important changes in the way you process customers. Three clients have told you they plan to use a competitor's service. You talked to your boss, but he refuses to make the changes saying, "This is the way it's always been done." You know your boss is coasting to retirement and not interested in rocking the boat. During an informal function you see your boss's boss and have an opportunity to share your concerns. What do you do?

How many times and in how many ways do we encounter these sticky situations at work? Whether our situation involves a colleague, our staff, our boss, or a client, each of us faces office dilemmas. What we do and how we respond can make or break our careers.

Successful people skills—the ability to communicate effectively in any situation—propel good leadership and teamwork. The ability to *say it just right* the first time without regrets and second thoughts enables leaders to climb up the ladder. We've all known and seen leaders who have this skill. We've watched them and thought, "I wish I could be like that" or "How did she know exactly what to say?" *Confidence* is the word that often comes to mind. These people appear confident in what they say and how they say it. That confidence inspires and attracts us.

Many books out there will tell you what to do in certain situations. They give excellent advice. For example Difalco and Herz's *The Big Sister's Guide to the World of Work*[1] contains real-life, down-to-earth tips for women in the workplace. The authors refresh and entertain us because they say, "Do it like this or else . . . ." Their lighthearted approach to tough situations, like asking for more money or interviewing for that perfect job, gives the average reader confidence that they, too, can *say it just right.* So . . . what's missing? How do you do it? How do those leaders you respect do it every time? Difalco and Herz tell you *what* to do but not *how.*

The authors of *Difficult Conversations*[2] provide another excellent example of what to do when conversations become difficult. After extensive research funded by the Harvard Negotiation Project, the authors dispense good advice about how to confront others. When conflicts arise at home or at work, they suggest ways to *say it just right.* Somewhere buried in the pages is a model, but where? Again, this book makes clear suggestions about what to do or what not to do but leaves the reader wondering how to do it.

In my search for not only what to do but how, I found a book with a clear formula. In *Working with You Is Killing Me*[3] Crowley and Elster not only tell you what to do but they suggest how. Unfortunately, the *how* grows like Jack's bean stalk as the book progresses. Instead of adhering to the original formula, they expand the formula as cases become stickier. By the end of the book, average readers scratch their heads and still wonder how to *say it just right.*

Seamless, fluid communication does not come easily to most of us. According to Susan RoAne in *How to Work a Room,*[4] 93 percent of us describe ourselves as shy. That means most of us would rather fade away than *say it just right.* We'd rather not stand up to the office bullies. We'd rather run away than maintain high ethical standards in the midst of toxic workplaces. *Managing Sticky Situations at Work* gives you a formula that you can use to *say it just right.* We pay close attention to what other authors suggest and build on their advice to illustrate the formula.

My mother taught me you can't have your cake and eat it, too. If we want to be successful, confident communicators, we must put ourselves forward and *say it just right.* This book provides the communication tools you need that will enable you to lead your department or your company into a more successful future. You will be the person others look at with admiring eyes. You will have the competitive edge in this increasingly tough job market.

The Say It Just Right™ (SIJR) Model combines *what* to do with *how* to do it. The pages that follow introduce you to the communication secrets for success in the workplace: First the **Three C's** (Change, Compassion, Curiosity) comprise the foundation for the model; next the **Decision Points** (Costs, Limits, Power) hammer in the framework; and finally the **SIJR Conversation** (Specify the Problem, Invite the Other Person to Talk, Join Feelings with Facts, Resolve the Issue) demonstrates how to *say it just right*. In Chapter 2 we examine how personality types affect the SIJR Model. The remaining chapters present scenarios from people in the workplace all over the world. When you finish, you will experience what confident communicators experience every day, *how to say it just right the first time.*

Before we begin, however, discover your own sticky situation quotient.

FIND OUT YOUR STICKY SITUATION QUOTIENT

1. If you had a boss who promised you a job assignment and then gave it to someone else. Would you . . .

   a. Quit
   b. Threaten to quit.
   c. Tell him you're upset and discover the specific reasons you didn't get the promotion

2. If your boss won't listen to your ideas and you know that things need to change, would you . . .

   a. Quit
   b. Negotiate with your boss and explain if things don't change the company could lose business
   c. Talk to your boss's supervisor

3. If your friend asks you for a recommendation and you know your friend isn't qualified for the job, would you . . .

   a. Make the recommendation anyway
   b. Tell your friend you can't make the recommendation and explain why
   c. Conveniently forget and never make the recommendation

4. You supervise a group of people who are giving you a lot of trouble. They deliberately withhold information from you and scheme to undermine your authority. Would you ...
   a. Talk to each individually to determine what can be done
   b. Fire them all and start over
   c. Try and befriend them

5. The group you supervise routinely conducts informal meetings without you. You've noticed that one person instigates the meetings. Do you ...
   a. Fire or reassign that person
   b. Attend the informal meetings uninvited
   c. Talk to the instigator and proceed with disciplinary measures if necessary

6. One of your fellow sales managers steals your prospects. You've seen him lurking around your desk and caught him when he contacted one of your prime buyers. Would you ...
   a. Immediately report him to your supervisor
   b. Steal his prospects
   c. Confront him

7. During an important job interview, the interviewer makes a lewd, clearly illegal comment. Would you ...
   a. Tell him the comment was offensive
   b. Pretend you didn't hear it
   c. Forget that job and search elsewhere, but tell everyone you know about it

8. One of your clients owes you money. You know that his business has been suffering in recent months. He's been a good client, but he's never paid you. Would you ...
   a. Write it off and quit doing business with him
   b. Bill him again with a note asking him to pay
   c. Talk to him and try to work out a payment plan

Answer key: Please see Appendix 1.

Your sticky situation quotient tells you whether you tend to turn away from sticky situations, whether you act passive-aggressively by indirectly responding to the situation, or whether you, in fact, deal directly with the problem. The higher your score the more likely it is you already deal directly with sticky situations and the more easily you'll apply the SIJR Model.

Before we embark on the communication secrets for success in the workplace and the SIJR Model, let's take a close look at communication.

NOTES

1. Marcelle Difalco and Jocelyn Greenky Herz, *The Big Sister's Guide to the World of Work* (New York: A Fireside Book, Simon & Schuster, 2005).

2. Douglas Stone, Bruce Patton, and Sheila Heen, *Difficult Conversations: How to Discuss What Matters Most* (New York: Penguin Books, 2000).

3. Katherine Crowley and Kathi Elster, *Working with You Is Killing Me* (New York: Warner Business Books, 2006).

4. Susan RoAne, *How to Work a Room: Your Essential Guide to Savvy Socializing* (New York: Collins, 2007), 3.

Chapter 1

The Say It Just Right™ (SIJR) Model

COMMUNICATION DEFINED

Years ago I uncovered a definition of communication that I doubt would appear in Wikipedia. I like it because of its simplicity as well as its inherent complexity.

Communication is behavior that transmits meaning from one person to another person.[1]

This definition tells us that we cannot communicate without behavior. We must *do* something to communicate. It also tells us that communication does not happen unless *meaning* is transmitted. Of course what I mean and what you think I mean pose two entirely different things. In fact, I can name at least six messages in any conversation.

- What you *Mean* to say
- What you *Actually* say
- What the other person *Hears*
- What the other person *Thinks* he/she hears

- What the other person *Says*

- What you *Think* the other person says

No wonder we encounter so many sticky communication problems. To make matters worse, did you know that our minds think *four* times faster than the average person can speak? Even when we *try* to listen, our thinking minds fly many miles an hour in another direction. Harnessing all that thinking energy takes discipline, focus, and concentration. In today's world where most of us multitask our way through life, stopping to really hear another person seems impossible. As we examine communication, you will see how important it is to stop doing whatever it is you are doing, to set your antenna in the direction of the speaker, and to assign your thinking mind the job of listening. Besides turning off our cell phones, however, how can we do this?

One way to compensate for these communication challenges is through good *feedback*. Feedback unravels these multiple messages and helps us focus our fast-thinking minds.

Great! Feedback solves the communication problem, right? Unfortunately, it's not quite that simple. One snag prevents feedback from being the communication savior. That snag lies in the question, Who assumes responsibility for the feedback—the person sending the message or the person receiving the message? Have you ever been in a meeting where no one takes charge? I'm sure you've had this experience and found it quite unpleasant. People float around, not sure what to do. Often these meetings produce nothing more than chaos and frustration. Because no one knows who is in charge of feedback, no one takes responsibility for feedback, and that creates chaos, frustration, and miscommunication.

We glean one lesson from this, particularly when we find ourselves in a sticky situation that involves tangled communication: We must take responsibility for feedback. Regardless of whether you send the message or receive it, *you* are responsible for feedback. As the sender, you must solicit feedback from your receiver. As the receiver, you must disclose or give feedback to your sender.

People often ask, "How do I solicit information if I'm not sure how the message was received?" The answer to this question requires you to tune up and sharpen your nonverbal antenna. When you see a frown, respond. When you hear a tentative quiver in the voice, notice it. Confident communicators, who *say it just right*, react to how the receiver responds to the message. They listen to not only what is said but also watch what is transmitted beyond the words, the nonverbal cues.

VERBAL AND NONVERBAL COMMUNICATION

According to landmark research done by Albert Mehrabian at UCLA in the 1960s,[2] there are three distinct parts that comprise communication: Visual, Vocal, and Verbal. Studying massive numbers of people over a series of years, he found that these three components impact our messages differently. Visual communication gives the message more power than vocal communication, and vocal gives the message more power than verbal. If you skip, ignore, or shortchange one of these three components, your message suffers.

By visual communication we mean *all the messages you get through the eyes*: gestures, facial expressions, eye contact, personal appearance. Dr. Mehrabian found that 55 percent of communication comes through visual messages.

By vocal communication *we mean all the non-word sounds we make* (including silence): um's, sighs, laughs, chuckles, grunts, groans. Vocal also includes articulation, modulation, pacing. Dr. Mehrabian found that 38 percent of communication comes through the ears.

By verbal communication we mean *the words* or the content of the message. Only 7 percent of communication comes through the content.

In one of my workshops someone said, "But, that's not right! We should pay more attention to the words than we do the actions." Perhaps we should. But, do we? Ask any politician or anyone in the broadcast industry. They will confirm the importance of visual and vocal (i.e., nonverbal) communication. There are people who make a living preparing defendants for jury trials. They do not tell them what to say but how to say it and how to "appear." When we talk about nonverbal communication, we mean the combination of the visual and vocal messages (93 percent). Confident communicators hear the words, and they heed the nonverbal cues. From those cues they discover the feelings behind the words.

What nonverbal cues do you notice in this sticky situation?

> *Roger is heading for a dinner meeting with one of his newest clients. He recently sold her an innovative computer software system. She requested that they get together to discuss the rollout in her company.*

Roger walks into the restaurant and finds Sandra seated at a table. She is holding a glass of wine. When he enters, she smiles and lifts her glass to him. "We should celebrate our new relationship and many more years of work together," she says. Roger smiles and agrees. He pulls out a chair across from her. In a small, almost imperceptible movement, she slides her chair toward his. "Drinks are on me," she says.

The waiter, who is standing ready, nods to Roger, who orders a glass of soda. Sandra raises an eyebrow. "Come on, Roger, relax. Have a drink with me to celebrate." She leans toward him and clicks her glass on his water glass. Roger agrees to one glass of white wine. He pulls out his laptop and clicks onto the software introductory proposal. Sandra brushes the hair from her forehead and says, "For heaven sakes, before we get into all that, I'd like to learn more about you. Tell me what you like to do when you're not working?" Her eyes bore into him.

How might you interpret the nonverbal messages Sandra sent to Roger?

- Her signals suggest anything from a simple relaxed friendship to a possible seduction.

- She encourages him with smiles, raised eyebrow, movement in his direction, informal touching of her hair.

- Her words say she wants to celebrate. Her actions suggest a little more.

How might you interpret the nonverbal messages Roger sent to Sandra?

- He sits across from her, not next to her, suggesting a formal meeting.

- He orders a nonalcoholic drink, suggesting he's working.

- He pulls out his laptop immediately. He wants to work.

When you find yourself in a situation where you communicate one type of relationship and the other person communicates another—and where the messages are primarily nonverbal—watch out.

As preamble to talking your way out of this sticky situation and avoiding the potential land mines, let's examine what makes communication successful. Even the best model will fail if we do not approach the situation effectively.

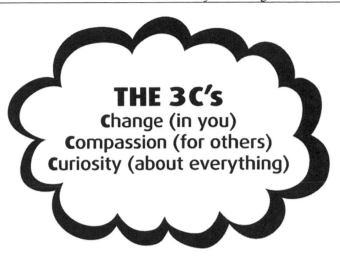

THE 3 C's
Change (in you)
Compassion (for others)
Curiosity (about everything)

The 3 C's

THE THREE C'S

To apply the SIJR Model we must consider the Three C's: *Change* is in you, *Compassion* for the other person, and *Curiosity* about everything.

CHANGE IS IN YOU

If you go into any communication with the intent to change another person, you will fail. Instead, communicate your wants and needs effectively and give the other person options. Of course you can suggest consequences if the behavior does not change, but the ultimate change decision lies with the other person. We know, however, that a person has a greater willingness to modify behavior when he or she perceives benefits. Salesmen know this quite well. They put themselves in the place of the buyer and wonder what the buyer wants, namely, how will this product or service benefit the buyer? As a confident communicator, you, too, must think about the benefits to the other person. How does life feel in that person's shoes? How does he see the world?

COMPASSION FOR THE OTHER PERSON

Assertiveness means "being able to say what you think and feel without stepping on other people's feet." In my view, Bower and Bower wrote one of the best books on assertiveness, *Asserting Yourself: A*

Practical Guide for Positive Change.[3] The authors present a practical model for making assertions in which they provide the communication tools to enable you to deal with sticky situations. Nonetheless, Bower and Bower leave out one critical ingredient, compassion. The authors do not consider the needs of the other person. In fact they refer to the other person as the "downer."

By contrast, in *Powerful Conversations: How High Impact Leaders Communicate*,[4] Paul Harkins talks about how leaders deepen trust. He created a model of trust that includes caring, commitment, and consistency. According to Harkins, communication does not exist without trust. He puts compassion and concern for the other person at the top of the list. He tells us that high-impact leaders "lead from the heart."[5]

CURIOSITY ABOUT EVERYTHING

Confident communicators come into the conversation with a healthy sense of curiosity. The wonderment that we found so refreshing as children seems to have faded with each year. Where did that wonder go? Confident communicators never lose the capacity to wonder. They realize that if they enter into a dialogue, knowing their own rightness, they miss an opportunity to learn. This does not mean short-changing your needs. It means listening to the needs of the other person with a third ear. As a communications coach, I experience the power of this kind of listening every day. The coaching literature defines[6] Level 1 listening as hearing from your point of view. Level 2 listening occurs when you hear the needs of the other person without going beyond the words. Level 3 listening goes beyond the words. Listening with the third ear means hearing what is not said and learning to read the nonverbal cues.

- Level 1 Listening response: "I understand where you are coming from. I've had a similar experience."

- Level 2 Listening response: "So you are saying you need more structure in your life."

- Level 3 Listening response: You notice the person's eyes moving as they talk. "I sense that you are preoccupied; what is disturbing you today?"

Before we return to Roger and Sandra, we must examine the second tier of the SIJR Model, namely, the Decision Points.

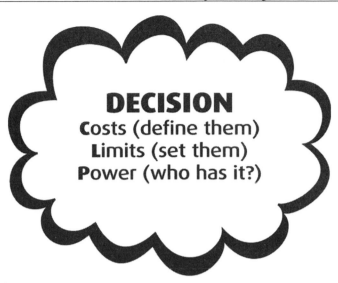

DECISION
Costs (define them)
Limits (set them)
Power (who has it?)

Decision Points

DECISION POINTS

Decision Points consist of three components: Defining the *Costs*, Setting your *Limits*, Determining the *Power Sources*. Confident communicators apply the Decision Points either before they initiate a conversation or after they've had an initial meeting. Some sticky situations are so sticky that you decide against confrontation. Knowing your own style of communication helps. Are you a direct communicator who often gets in trouble for talking and then thinking? Are you an indirect communicator who often goes around the problem to arrive at a solution? Are you a fearful communicator who thinks so long that you often lose the opportunity to speak?

HOW STRAIGHT A TALKER ARE YOU?

(Answer True or False)

1. When you have something to say, you should gather all the facts and all the information before you say it.
2. It is a good idea to tell people how you see their behavior is causing problems from what you've heard others say.
3. You should not express your own feelings when you want to say something; it just muddies the water.
4. When you describe what you think is wrong with someone, you should clearly describe the other person's behavior.

5. When you compliment someone, you don't need to be too specific.
6. When someone has a bad attitude, you should tell him right away so he can correct it.
7. If you feel yourself getting emotionally overwrought, you should table the conversation for later.
8. When talking to someone directly, you should not look at them in the eye.
9. You should use a lot of gestures to explain what you are saying.
10. It is not up to you to solve the problem. You should not present your ideas for a solution.

Answer Key: Please see Appendix 1.

Depending on your Straight Talker score, you will be more or less likely to jump into any communication. The *Decision Points* will guide you to either stop in your tracks or to persist.

DEFINE THE COST

What is the cost for saying or doing anything? In Roger's situation, he has a lot to lose. Sandra is a new client and one he's worked hard to land. He might say to himself, "I'm imagining all this. Maybe she's just being friendly. I should ignore her and press forward." If he takes that approach without directly confronting Sandra, he could send her the wrong message. We've seen how slippery communication can be. Roger takes a big risk with doing nothing. On the other hand, if Roger confronts Sandra too directly, he risks insulting her. In defining cost, we often overlook our own merit. Sandra bought Roger's product because it added value to her company. If he confronts her with genuine curiosity and compassion without making judgments about her, he can set limits within the framework of the Three C's. She, therefore, decides whether or not she'll sacrifice what benefit his product brings her company. In other words, she decides to change or not. Having confidence in your product, your service, or yourself gives you that extra edge to *say it*.

SET THE LIMITS

What are you willing to do or not do? Roger must clarify where he draws the line. Perhaps he is not willing to treat clients as "friends."

Once he sets his limits with Sandra, he can share those limits in a detached manner. It's not Sandra but Sandra the client he is talking to. Sandra may want to have a personal relationship with the people she does business with. Roger, on the other hand, prefers to keep the tone strictly professional.

DETERMINE THE POWER SOURCES

Who has the power? Are you feeling powerless? When we feel powerless, any situation becomes stickier. Roger feels powerless because he has given Sandra all the power. As the customer, she holds the purse strings. He fears she'll take away her business if he confronts her. That fear causes him to give up his power which she willingly accepts. Roger does not have to give up his power, however. What does Roger lose if Sandra pulls back her business? What does Sandra lose? Undoubtedly there is more to lose on both sides than either realize. Roger must reassert his position of power with the same confidence he showed when he sold Sandra the product. That reassertion will enable him to take the risk to clarify his position. From this vantage point Roger can say what he recommends will resolve the sticky situation and negotiate a solution that does not convey a sense of powerlessness on either side.

How might Roger reassert himself? He begins by posing powerful questions to Sandra. What does she hope to accomplish tonight? He should make it clear to her that although he is willing to celebrate their new *business* relationship, he wants to discuss the rollout. If Sandra persists in a way that makes Roger uncomfortable, he should indicate that he prefers meeting during office hours.

Let's examine another sticky situation and watch how a confident communicator applies the Three C's and the Decision Points.

> *Mary Lou's boss enters her cubical with the annual report and tosses it on her desk. "We need to get this out by the end of the day," he tells her. The clock reads nearly 4:30. Mary Lou has an appointment with her personal trainer at 5:30. She cannot finish that report and keep her appointment. She knows that her boss has had this document for several days and has put off finishing it. This isn't the first time he's saved something until the last minute and then expected her to stay late to get it out.*
>
> *"I have to tell you that I won't be able to finish this before 5:00, and I can't stay late tonight," Mary Lou says.*

"Listen, Mary Lou, I don't ask you to stay late often. This is important. I need to get it out right away."

"I recognize how important this is to you, but this particular night I can't stay late. What other options are available to us?"

"There are no other options," he responds.

Mary Lou takes a deep breath. "Help me understand what is going on here. What are the pressures that necessitate getting this out tonight and not tomorrow morning?"

"I just want it off my desk and out of my mind."

"So," she says, "you really don't have to have it out tonight. You're just tired of thinking about it and want to get rid of it?"

Her boss's eyes shift and he sighs: "The problem is it's overdue, and I promised Jake I'd get it done tonight. I should have gotten it out last week."

"This report is obviously something that has been bothering you. What kinds of things got in the way of getting it out last week?" she asks.

"I simply hate doing this darn thing. I am not comfortable writing, and I tend to put it off for as long as I can."

"I like to write. Maybe next time I can help you with some of the parts you find difficult."

He smiles. "That would be great. But, what about this report? I really need it out tonight."

"The best I can offer is first thing tomorrow. Next time, why don't we plan to meet in early June and begin pulling the data together. Then I will write a draft for you, and we'll go from there. What do you think?"

"That's a good plan."

"In the future if you come to me sooner with projects that you don't like, maybe we can put our heads together and get it done with as little pain as possible. That way we won't get stuck at the last minute trying to finish and maybe disappointing Jake."

"I'll do my best, but sometimes I have to wait on data from other parts of the company," he says.

"If we get most of it done ahead of time, we can always fill in the blanks later. Meantime, I promise I'll get this report out first thing tomorrow."

There is no guarantee that Mary Lou's boss's behavior will change. Next year, he may still bring the report to her at the last minute. If he does, however, he knows to expect that it will go out late. She clearly set her limits. She listened to his needs from an orientation of curiosity and compassion and suggested a solution that would benefit him. Instead of being angry or upset with him for assuming she'd stay late to bail him out once again, she questioned him with genuine curiosity. Without judging him as a procrastinator, she learned the real reason he delayed getting the report to her.

Mary Lou shifted the power base. Even though she's the subordinate, she showed her value to her boss without allowing him to intimidate her.

Mary Lou is on the road to becoming a confident communicator who knows how to *say it just right*.

Say It Just Right™ Conversation

Now that we know the basics of communication, understand the Three C's for successful communication, and recognize the need to apply the Decision Points, we can *say it just right*.

The components of the SIJR Conversation consist of four parts: *Specify* the Problem, *Invite* the Other Person to Talk, *Join* Feelings with Facts, *Resolve* the Issue. When one part is omitted, the power of the message decreases.

Specify the Problem

When you describe the problem, make sure you identify in specific terms what bothers you or what you believe to be true. Do not talk

CONVERSATION
Specify (the problem)
Invite (others to talk)
Join Feelings + Facts
Resolve Issues

SIJR Conversation

in general terms, talk in behavioral terms. *What did the other person do?* Can you see the behavior? Telling someone you don't like his attitude is not specific. How can you see an attitude?

Going back to our example with Roger and Sandra, let's look at how each might specify the problem from his or her different viewpoints:

Roger to Sandra: "It concerns me that you want me to have a drink while we are conducting business."

Sandra to Roger: "It bothers me that you always pull out your laptop and get right to work before you even say 'hello.' "

Some tips:

- Say directly and specifically the problem you see. Do not describe how you think the other person sees the problem. Instead, specify the problem in your own terms from your own perspective. You want to avoid using words that might cause defensiveness or that sound as if you blame the other person.

- Talk in "I" versus "You" messages. I-messages tend to keep the communication less threatening and explosive. You-messages cause defensiveness. When I say, "*You* make me angry or *you* hurt my feelings," I'm using you-messages. Initiate the conversation from the standpoint of "I." This doesn't mean that every statement must start with the word "I."

Roger to Sandra   *Wrong way:* "You make me feel nervous by asking me to talk about things that are not work related."   *Right way:* "I'm a private person, and it makes me uncomfortable to talk with clients about things that don't relate to work."

Sandra to Roger   *Wrong way:* "You're so uptight. Why don't you relax?"   *Right way:* "I like to build rapport with the people I work with. I'm not comfortable doing business with strangers."

INVITE THE OTHER PERSON TO TALK

Dialogue forms the best kind of communication. According to Stone et al., in *Difficult Conversations,* begin your conversation with what they refer to as the Third Story. "The Third Story is the one a keen observer would tell."[7] Instead of beginning the conversation with your story or with the story you *think* the other person might tell, begin where you believe an impartial mediator would start. As a mediator myself, I learned how to really listen with an impartial ear to each point of view. Mediators struggle to be detached because it is very hard not to let your biases and expectations color what you are hearing. You can do this, however, when you use the Say It Just Right Model because you communicate with *curiosity* and wonder. By inviting the other person to "tell his story," you listen with curiosity to the way he sees and perceives things. You take that information and combine it with your own. What comes out is the Third Story.

Notice in our earlier example with Mary Lou and her boss that she asked for her boss's story when she said, "What kinds of things got in the way of getting the report out last week?" She listened to his response with that neutral, unbiased ear, noting his concern and not judging him.

Join Feelings with Facts

Feelings humanize what we say. When I hear sadness, hurt, or disappointment, I know I'm dealing with a person. When I know I'm dealing with a person, I am less likely to attack. Be as straightforward with your feelings as you are when you express behaviors and avoid getting "emotional" or using highly charged words.

Example: *Wrong way:* "You make me mad by never telling me when you are leaving." *Right way:* "It frustrates me when you leave without telling me. It makes me feel as if what I'm doing does not matter to you."

Remember that your feelings show through in your nonverbal behaviors. When you do not say what you feel, people still know it. To say it just right you want the feelings you express and the feelings you show to match. Thousands of nonverbal behaviors bombard our communication all the time. Being aware of your visual and vocal cues will add credibility to your message.

Some quick tips:

- Look the person in the eye, but don't stare them down.
- Stand erect. Don't shift from foot to foot.
- Avoid scowls or frowns that show displeasure.
- Don't fiddle with pens, pencils, or cell phones.
- Smile when you mean it; don't smile when you don't.
- Eliminate the "um's" and "ah's."
- Use gestures to punctuate your main points.

RESOLVE THE ISSUE

No one likes a complainer. Be willing to negotiate and look for resolutions. Listen to the ideas the other person suggests.

Say a boss calls on you and embarrasses you in meetings. "Now that we've both shared what we think the problem is, what do you think will help us resolve it?" you ask. Once you've listened to your boss's ideas, you can insert your own, for example: "It would really help me prepare, and I'd be less embarrassed, if you would warn me before you called on me during the meeting."

One tip when looking for resolution is to include what will happen if we do nothing or if things remain the same. This component specifies consequences to the other person if they choose not to change their behavior. Ideally you want to show the benefits of change, rather than the punishments for not changing. Sometimes, however, you have no choice but to show the negative consequences. Regardless of whether you choose positive or negative consequences, if the person elects not to change, you must follow through. In other words if you say, "If I don't get a salary adjustment by the end of this quarter, I will leave the company," and your boss responds that he cannot guarantee the salary adjustment, you must make good on what you said. You cannot backtrack. Otherwise you will lose all credibility in future conversations.

Let's look at how Roger applies the SIJR Model in his conversation with Sandra. He outlines these Decision Points:

- Before he talks to Sandra he sets his limits: He will not meet after hours unless no other time is available to the two of them.

- He determines the cost: If he loses Sandra's business, his company will survive. He must find another major client this year, but several opportunities do exist.

- He shifts the power: After rerunning the numbers, which he used to sell his system to Sandra, he recognizes how much value his product adds to her company. He feels confident she will not want to sacrifice her company based on his desire to meet formally rather than informally.

SAY IT JUST RIGHT CONVERSATION

Seated in Sandra's office, Roger says, "Sandra, I am very excited to be joining your team. I reran the numbers last night and have more data to show you that indicate how valuable our product will be to your company. I predict quick results. But, I must tell you I am uncomfortable meeting outside the office. I'm curious to know, from your viewpoint, how do you want us to work together?" (**He specified the problem, invited her to talk, and joined feelings with fact.**)

Sandra taps her desk with her finger. "I'm not sure I understand what you mean."

"I'm talking about the meeting last night over dinner. That kind of out-of-office meeting troubles me, and I'm wondering how you felt." (**He is showing curiosity and compassion and not asking her to change.**)

Sandra smiles. "Obviously you've never worked with a family-owned company. In our business everyone is family. We talk about embracing our employees and customers. I've always maintained a very warm office environment."

Roger uncrosses his legs and shifts forward. "You're right. I haven't worked for a company that's as chummy as you describe. Most are pretty stiff. I guess my style is pretty stiff, too. After all, I'm a techie." Sandra laughs and he does, too. "How can we deal with this issue? I want to be responsive to you, but it's hard for me when I feel uncomfortable." (**He is asking for her ideas to resolve the issue.**)

Sandra says, "I realize that our company culture might be a little off-putting to some people. I really like what your product can do for us and am willing to explore what we can work out." She sighs. " Let's see. Why don't we meet for coffee once a month? Is a coffee meeting too intimate for you?"

Roger responds: "That sounds great. I'll try to be more relaxed and maybe as I get used to your style, it will be easier. But, evening meetings are just not going to work for me." (**The resolution sounds good to him and he restates his limits.**)

Sandra: "I get it. No worries."

They set a time for their next morning meeting.

Roger shakes Sandra's hand before leaving. "I'm glad we talked about this. I want our business relationship to flourish, and I don't want any misunderstandings." (**He ends with positive consequences.**)

In this chapter we've laid the foundation for the SIJR Model. We examined the Three C's (change, compassion, and curiosity) and the Decision Points (costs, limits, and power). We also introduced the SIJR Conversation. Before we look at other sticky situations in which we will apply the SIJR Model, we must examine one additional issue: how different personality types affect communication.

NOTES

1. Richard Huseman, *Readings in Business Communication: Strategies and Skills* (Hinsdale, IL: Dryden Press, 1981).

2. Albert Mehrabian and Morton Weiner, *Language Within Language* (New York: Appleton-Century-Crofts, 1968).

3. Sharon Anthony Bower and Gorden H. Bower, *Asserting Yourself: A Practical Guide for Positive Change* (Reading, MA: Perseus Books, 1991).

4. Phil Harkins, *Powerful Conversations: How High Impact Leaders Communicate* (New York: McGraw Hill, 1999), 98.

5. Ibid., 75.

6. Laura Whitworth, Karen Kimsey-House, Henry Kimsey-House, and Phillip Sandahl, *Co-Active Coaching: New Skills for Coaching People toward Success in Work and Life* (Mountain View, CA: Davies-Black Publishing, 2007), 34–36.

7. Douglas Stone, Bruce Patton, and Sheila Heen, *Difficult Conversations: How to Discuss What Matters Most* (New York: Penguin Books, 2000), 149–50.

Chapter 2

Personality Overlay

At this stage we understand the SIJR Model, and we have observed how it works. We are now ready to apply it to sticky situations. Hold on! If we faced cardboard people every day, who always acted the same way, we could apply the SIJR Model right now. Unfortunately (some may say fortunately) people are different. These differences require that we not only understand what to say and how to say it, but also to whom we are saying it.

Crowley and Elster in *Working with You Is Killing Me* handle this problem nicely. They describe seven different personalities and suggest ideas about what to do when faced with these different people.[1] According to the first of the Three C's we cannot change the other person. We must, therefore, adjust our style whenever we face a different personality. Crowley and Elster come from this orientation. They suggest ideas about how to "unhook" from the bad place these personalities put us in and regain control.[2]

PERSONALITY OVERLAY DEFINED

The Three C's comprise the foundation to the SIJR Model, and the Decision Points provide the framework. The Personality Overlay

Personality Overlay

colors in the background behind the picture. Imagine a photo of the forum in ancient Rome as we see it today with the rocks, columns, pieces of statuary, and gravel foot paths. Visualize an overlay that depicts the way ancient Rome looked centuries ago with intact buildings, temples, magnificent statues, and elaborate houses. That overlay shows us the full picture. Without that overlay we cannot envision the way things were. Similarly, when dealing with sticky situations, we encounter people who overlay reactions to the events around them. We must consider these people and their unique personality styles before we embark on a SIJR Conversation.

Unlike Crowley and Elster's model, the SIJR Model remains intact even when we adjust our style to accommodate different personalities. We begin with the Decision Points in order to decide whether to have a conversation and if so, how to prepare ourselves for the limitations and risks. Given each personality we must adjust our SIJR Conversation accordingly. To simplify our analysis of personality, we selected the styles created by James Brewer et al. in *Power Management: A Three-Step Program for Successful Leadership.*[3]

Brewer created a simple but effective survey to determine personality style. Unlike some of the more popular assessments, such as Myers-Briggs—whose styles baffle us and often disappear from our memories (ENFJ [extrovert intuitive, feeling, judging], ISTP [introvert, sensing, thinking, perceiving]), Brewer's style types are easy to identify: Bold, Expressive, Sympathetic, and Technical (BEST).[4] Furthermore, if you cannot administer the My BEST Profile,[5] you can quickly observe behaviors and deduce one of the styles.

BOLD PERSONALITY TYPE

Stewart works as a physician's assistant in a large hospital. The medical director, Dr. Holmes, is one of the top general surgeons in the country. Stewart enjoys working under Dr. Holmes because he respects his quality work. Dr. Holmes demands perfection from everyone around him. He sometimes will bite off the heads of nurses when he feels they do not do what he wants fast enough. Once when Stewart was preparing a patient for surgery, Dr. Holmes barged into the room. He said to Stewart, "This patient must be ready in five minutes. We are already late for surgery." Stewart spent the next 10 minutes calming the patient. Even though Dr. Holmes demands a lot, everyone recognizes his skill and his ability to keep things running smoothly. Dr. Holmes never compliments anyone's work. He finishes his part of the procedure, turns, and leaves without a word to anyone. One morning when Stewart saw him in the hall, he said, "Good morning, Dr. Holmes." Holmes responded, "Not now, Stewart, make an appointment." Stewart laughed. "Must I make an appointment to say 'good morning'?" That incident became a hospital legend.

Stewart works for a Bold personality type. Furthermore, he has learned how to adjust his style in order to work with Dr. Holmes. He does not expect Dr. Holmes to spend time talking to him, to ask about his family, or to compliment his work. He would expect Dr. Holmes, however, to pounce on him if he made a careless error. Stewart has modified his own style in the face of Dr. Holmes. By so doing, he does not expect more of Dr. Holmes than his Bold personality can deliver.

Action drives Bolds. They make quick decisions, focus on results, compete with everyone, show determination to the point of stubbornness, and love to multitask. They communicate in short sentences without elaboration or clarification. They look at their watches frequently and come to meetings on time or early. They demand fast results from subordinates. They prefer not to work on teams because teamwork wastes time (in their view). The Bold person loves challenges and adventure. A group of Bolds often jump to a quick decision within minutes of getting a task and then spend the rest of their time looking for new tasks.

EXPRESSIVE PERSONALITY TYPE

Sandi coordinates a large cultural program for an upscale residential community. She goes to national meetings and recruits top-notch personalities to her events. She hobnobs with her target audience to learn more about what activities they might enjoy. Sandi operates in fast-forward—always on the run, spending more time in her brochure-stuffed car than her office. She collects information about new talent and stores boxes of media spreads in her trunk. When she meets people, she talks up the programs she has created and the beauty of the residential facility where she works. Her quick, talkative, engaging style draws others to her. Her natural optimism enables her to see opportunity around every corner.

Marsha works as Sandi's assistant. Marsha can only reach Sandi by cell phone because Sandi is rarely in her office. These phone conversations frustrate Marsha because of the background noise as well as Sandi's on-the-run, multitasking style. Sandi designs and organizes each of the programs, but once they are finished, she launches off to create a new one. Marsha steps in to manage all the details. She sets up sufficient chairs for participants, provides adequate food, checks and rechecks the audio visuals, and creates eye-pleasing amenities that make each event special. At the last minute Sandi and the guest speaker arrive. They invariably change things Marsha has done. Marsha knows that no amount of preparation will eliminate Sandi's need to put her mark on how things are set up on the day of the event.

Marsha works for an Expressive personality type. Sandi thrives on being around people, conversing with others, and soaking up the limelight. Marsha knows that she cannot pin Sandi down. She must catch Sandi on Sandi's terms in order to find out how to set up each event. Not having unrealistic expectations, Marsha anticipates that there will be changes the night of the event. She knows that all the preparation in the world will not stop Sandi from rearranging the chairs, asking for different tablecloths or resetting the head table, often in view of the guest speaker. This need of Sandi's has nothing to do with Marsha's work.

People stimulate Expressives. They engage others with enthusiasm and a positive attitude. They enjoy going to meetings but often arrive late. When they enter a room, everyone notices them. A buzz of energy seems to follow them. Expressives dress in bold colors—reds, yellows, oranges. They initiate greetings by quickly saying hello and shaking hands. Although engaging, they lose interest when you talk about your family or other personal issues. They prefer to tell you all about themselves and their projects. A group of Expressives struggles when asked to complete a task because each must talk. Instead of listening to one another, however, they vie for center stage. At the end of the work time, the group reports that they enjoyed themselves, but they did not reach a firm decision.

SYMPATHETIC PERSONALITY TYPE

Jonathan works as a financial advisor in a large investment bank. Each morning he enters his building, says hello to the guard, and asks him about his recently hospitalized wife. On the way to his 10th floor cubicle, he stops at the coffee shop for a light breakfast. There he visits with two other financial advisors who work on the floor beneath him. He tells them about what he has just read in the Wall Street Journal *concerning the latest market trends. One says that he gives away too much information. Jonathan responds, "We all help each other out. That's why we have the best investment bank in the world." Jonathan's boss enters the coffee shop. He sits down next to Jonathan with his Blackberry in hand. "I'm not sure I can get through all this," he says, scrolling down his daily to-do list. "Can I help with any of that?" Jonathan asks. His boss turns over one project and says, "Sure you don't mind?" Jonathan smiles. "No problem. You always come through for me. Consider this my thanks." Before his boss leaves, he asks Jonathan to give him the latest earnings reports. "They are already done. I'll e-mail them to you when I get to my desk," Jonathan replies.*

Jonathan embodies a Sympathetic personality. Loyal and unselfish, he does not hesitate to help others so long as he respects and trusts them. Most people find him easy to be around because of his generosity and concern for them. His compassion shows in his ability to listen whenever people share problems, home or work related. A group of Sympathetics accomplish whatever task you might give them. They like to please. Rather than take risks or think outside the box, they toe the line in order to win the praise of their leaders.

Sympathetics thrive on appreciation. They do what they believe you want. Perhaps you can't imagine a sticky situation with a Sympathetic. One of the most difficult things you may encounter in your career is to give a good, loyal, obedient Sympathetic low performance measures or to inform a Sympathetic that his job is no longer available. Imagine Jonathan's boss in such a situation. If he treats Jonathan with respect, honesty, and compassion, the enormity of the task diminishes. Offering to give Jonathan a good reference or to make some calls on his behalf also goes far with Sympathetics like Jonathan.

TECHNICAL PERSONALITY TYPE

Joanne manages a team of IT professionals in a large computer-based firm. These people create new software packages aimed at implementing technology. Larry works for Joanne and has been acknowledged as one of the brightest people on her team. During the last two years he has won awards for his creative, technical expertise. Larry organizes and conceptualizes his work with great care. Whatever he submits to Joanne exceeds her expectations. Larry prefers working individually to working with the team. Nonetheless, he attends meetings and delivers any information that others request of him. Joanne has one problem with Larry. The company requires that everyone submit timesheets. These sheets make no sense to Joanne's team because people do not work a regimented 8:00 to 5:00 day. As salaried employees, not hourly or contractual, they receive the same stipend regardless of the number of hours worked. The company, however, insists on time-sheet compliance. Joanne has begged Larry to complete his time-sheets. He says, "I don't have time to do that Mickey-Mouse work. I'm working on creating a new system and not on filling in hours on a sheet that really doesn't matter." Joanne agrees but explains that her boss will come down on the whole team if the sheets are not completed and signed. On the day before the timesheet deadline, Joanne sent the following e-mail to Larry:

> *There once was a tech named Larry*
> *Who was so good it was just scary*
> *But his timesheet was late*
> *So he suffered the fate*
> *Of bad poetry sent to his Blackberry[6]*

Once he received that e-mail, he completed his timesheet and has done so each quarter since.

Larry is clearly a Technical personality type. Being logical, organized, cautious, and systematic, he sees no point in doing the timesheets. In Larry's mind the timesheet exercise wastes time, and that's illogical. Joanne searched for a way to get to Larry. Using the company compliance rationale did not affect him. Furthermore, Larry's cautious nature prevented him from signing a form that distorted his real work time. By tapping into Larry's creative energy and using humor, Joanne found a way to deal with Larry's technical personality and win his compliance to what everyone agreed posed a useless endeavor.

Technicals operate by the rules. They search for organization and logic. Often you can identify Technical personalities by the state of their offices. Technicals carefully label files and line pens up in perfect order. They prefer to work alone rather than in teams. When they must work in teams, they tend to hold back rather than become fully interdependent team members. If you put a group of Technicals together on a project, it bogs down because no one steps up to make a decision, and each holds back, preferring not to share his or her true views.

APPLYING THE SIJR MODEL

Let's look at a sticky situation and apply the SIJR Model in view of the BEST personality styles.

Lewis works as the HR manager in a large car manufacturing company. He supervises 14 people. Lewis began as an employment interviewer 14 years ago and moved up through the ranks to the top position. One of his longtime subordinates, Nancy, spends too much time visiting outside the department. Her peers complain about her frequent disappearances. Even though people throughout the company like her, Nancy produces adequate, but not outstanding work. Furthermore, she's been known to have a loose tongue. With recent downsizing in his company, Lewis must allocate time very carefully. The department cut back to 15 percent fewer people this year, and Lewis expects more cuts next year. Penny, one of Lewis's most valued employees, recently complained that Nancy divulged information about a pending grievance to someone in another department.

Lewis hates confrontations. He has avoided unpleasant conversations with Nancy in the past because he'd hoped things would work out. He realizes now that she has crossed the line.

DECISION POINTS

Lewis sets limits. Nancy cannot violate employee confidentiality.

Lewis determines the costs. Although Nancy has worked for the company for a long time and people all the way up the chain like her, he could replace her. With less than stellar performance evaluations, Lewis can justify beginning disciplinary actions which could lead to her dismissal. Nonetheless, he, too likes Nancy, and if she changes her behavior, he will do what he can to keep her.

Lewis looks at the power source. Nancy protects herself with her good relationships throughout the company as well as with her intimate knowledge of the grievance procedures. Lewis, nonetheless, also enjoys good relationships with people in the company. He realizes, however, that many people will fight on Nancy's behalf if he decides to release her.

SAY IT JUST RIGHT CONVERSATION

Lewis invites Nancy to come see him at 9:00 the following morning.

"I appreciate your coming to see me. I'm concerned about an incident regarding one of our cases and wanted to hear your side about what happened," Lewis begins.

"What are you talking about? I can't think of what incident someone complained to you about. I just try and do as I'm told."

"I'm referring to the Sam Smith case and aspects of that case that you shared with your friend John, in marketing. I'm frustrated because this is not the first time you have talked to people outside our department about cases we are dealing with. You know how much we depend on confidentiality. I'm curious to know what happened to make you share sensitive information about a case with John." (**Specifies the problem, joins feeling with fact, and invites Nancy to talk.**)

"John already knew about the case. He approached me even before the employee came to talk to us. I encouraged John to tell Sam to come see me. What's more John knows a lot about what is going on in the company. I thought he could shed some light on what happened since he's friendly with Sam. Anyway, all I did was tell him we managed to fend off a lawsuit."

Lewis focuses on Nancy. "John works in marketing. He really does not have anything to do with our cases. I'm curious to know how you thought John would help you." (**Lewis demonstrates genuine curiosity.**)

"John knows Sam better than I do. He gave me some good advice about how to deal with him. I like to find out what makes people tick before I talk to them. John's suggestions helped me be more understanding and persuasive. I really think without his help, I would not have been as successful with Sam."

"So what you are saying is that John's input guided you in your conversation with the employee. What about after you met with Sam? I understand you shared sensitive information with John afterwards?" **(Respecifies the problem.)**

"He just asked how it went." She looks away. "Sometimes I say more than I should. I tend to get carried away, and I was so excited to have that case resolved. John was a huge help. I guess I might have told him more about what happened than I should have. Honestly, though, I don't think I violated the employee's confidentiality."

"Just talking with John about a pending case constitutes a violation. I'm disappointed that you did this. Perhaps I had not made our policy clear enough to you. I should have talked to you about this long ago. Since John is not in HR, he has told others about this case and now it is general knowledge. How can we prevent this kind of thing from happening in the future?" **(Clarifies the problem and solicits ideas for resolution.)**

Nancy looks down: "I guess I need to stay in my office and not talk to so many people."

Lewis smiles. "Really, Nancy, I don't see that happening. You are a very engaging person, and you like interacting with others. I doubt trying to shut yourself away in your office will work. What other ideas might work?" **(Looks for resolution.)**

She turns away. "Well . . . I suppose I can be more careful when talking with people outside our department. I don't think I violated confidentiality, but it could appear that way. Next time, once a case is in our hands, I will tell John I can't talk about it."

"I know how much you like to visit with people, and you have a very friendly style. We like that in HR. But, you have to be careful not to go over the line. It could jeopardize your career. I want you to be successful in your work, and I also want you to enjoy what you do."

"I do enjoy my work."

"I'm glad. In the future, watch yourself when you talk to people outside this department. If this kind of information leaks again, I will have to put a warning in your personnel file. I hope I won't have to do that." **(Specifies positive and negative consequences.)**

ANALYSIS

What personality style was Lewis dealing with? Nancy likes to talk. She enjoys being with people. She exudes a friendly manner. In all likelihood she's an Expressive. As an Expressive, Lewis recognized that she could not stop visiting with people. Furthermore, her job requires her to know and interact with a lot of people in the company. But, she cannot share confidential information with her friends. Lewis remained firm, but he showed compassion and curiosity. In the end, he doesn't know if Nancy will change her behavior, but he made it clear what will happen if she does not.

Specify the Problem. She violated confidentiality about a current case.

Invite the Other Person to Talk. Nancy wanted to talk right away, and that typifies her Expressive style. Lewis listened to her rationale and tried to understand her position.

Join Feelings with Fact. Lewis told her he was disappointed with her behavior and concerned about what happened.

Say It Just Right Model

Resolve the Issue: Nancy came up with her own resolution, namely, she promised not to talk about current cases with people outside the department. To nail down the resolution Lewis specified two consequences, one positive and one negative. He intimated that if she changed her behavior, she could become more successful in her job. On the other hand, if she continued talking about cases outside the department, he would begin disciplinary procedures.

To summarize the SIJR Model: The Decision Points (costs, limits, power sources) determine whether we begin a conversation and if we do, what limitations and risks we face. The Three C's (change, compassion, and curiosity) hold the model together because they keep us focused and oriented toward a positive and realistic solution. Together the Decision Points and the Three C's tell us *what* to say. The SIJR Conversation (specify the problem, invite the other person to talk, join feelings with facts, resolve the issue) guides us in *how* to say it. As we saw in this chapter, Personality Overlay assures a successful outcome by taking into account *to whom* we are saying it.

Some of the stickiest situations we face are those that deal with our bosses. The next chapter examines how the SIJR Model works in these kinds of encounters.

NOTES

1. Katherine Crowley and Kathi Elster, *Working with You Is Killing Me* (New York: Warner Business Books, 2006), 70–72.

2. Ibid., 4–10.

3. James H. Brewer, J. Michael Ainsworth, and George E. Wynne, *Power Management: A Three-Step Program for Successful Leadership* (Englewood Cliffs, NJ: Prentice Hall, 1984).

4. James H. Brewer, Associated Consultants in Education, 1989.

5. To order My BEST Profile go to www.hrdq.com.

6. Joanne Shortell limerick, www.shortellcoaching.com. The incident has been altered and the names changed.

Chapter 3

Sticky Situations with Your Boss

At some point in our lives, we stumble upon a boss who is difficult to work with. When you find yourself in this situation, you must first decide if your boss is difficult with everyone or merely with you.

If the boss is difficult with everyone, you are dealing with a *Difficult Person*. The way you deal with a Difficult Person differs from the way you might deal with a boss who is difficult only with you. When you and your boss clash, you have a personality conflict. You can apply the SIJR Model in both instances. When you apply the model with a Difficult Person, however, some tips might guide you.

TIPS FOR DEALING WITH A DIFFICULT PERSON

- Don't take the difficult behavior personally. Be aware that your boss clashes with everyone, not just you. Recognize the individual's inability to relate to other people as his or her problem, not yours.

- Don't get defensive, even if you have to bite your tongue. When you defend yourself, the Difficult Person wins. Instead, ignore comments that put you on the defensive and stay on track. Defer to the SIJR Model to help you remain detached. For example, concentrate on using "I" messages versus "You" messages. Or, concentrate on being curious.

- Look for positive qualities in the Difficult Person. Perhaps that person excels at details; perhaps he or she handles crises well. Capitalize on these qualities when you deal with the Difficult Person. Remember one component of the SIJR Model is compassion.

- Learn to cope with your own emotions. Difficult People drain your emotions. Give yourself opportunities to let emotions out. Try exercise, meditation, or fun activities with friends. Do not dump on your loved ones day after day. Search for other means to vent your frustrations.

- Learn to handle your own problems. The less interaction with the Difficult Person the better for all concerned.

When researching this book, I heard countless people describe their difficult bosses as sociopaths. I heard words like crazy, sick, mentally unstable. When you put this kind of label on someone, you give yourself permission to toss in the towel. How could you possibly deal with a crazy sociopath? The fault for everything that's gone wrong lies with your boss, right? Perhaps the boss is not as mentally imbalanced as you think. Perhaps you just did not *say it just right*.

ARE YOU A DIFFICULT PERSON?

Read each statement and rate it as truthfully as you can. Does the statement sound like something you'd say or do?

1. I can't wait to finish conversations with other people.
   Less True   1   2   3   4   5   More True

2. My staff tells me I'm a very demanding leader.
   Less True   1   2   3   4   5   More True

3. No one has ever told me how great it was to work for me.
   Less True   1   2   3   4   5   More True

4. When people tell me nice things, I know they want something.
   Less True   1   2   3   4   5   More True

5. Most people don't care about anything but doing as little as they can to get by.
   Less True   1   2   3   4   5   More True

6. I never bother my boss with little things. Why should others come to me when they can't do their jobs?
   Less True   1   2   3   4   5   More True

7. You have to have thick skin to work for me.
    Less True   1   2   3   4   5   More True
8. Most of what I do is fix other people's mistakes.
    Less True   1   2   3   4   5   More True

Score yourself in Appendix 1

STICKY SITUATION # 1:
"CAN'T YOU DO ANYTHING RIGHT?"

*Peter works for Angie. He knew when he went into the depart-
ment that Angie had a reputation as a difficult boss. Everyone
who has worked for her either left the company or transferred to
another division after less than a year. Angie runs the graphics
department in a large advertising agency. She uses intimidation
as her style of management. Peter graduated from a prestigious
university with an MFA. He's always felt comfortable about his
skill as an artist and as a creative designer. Working for Angie,
however, has shattered his confidence because he can't seem to satisfy her.*

*Today, Peter put the finishing touches on the design for a client
with whom he has an excellent relationship. He's met endlessly
with the client and his VP for marketing to get a clear understanding of what they want. The deadline for submitting a concept to the client is tomorrow. Peter braces himself because he
knows he needs Angie's okay. He knocks on her door frame.*

*"For heaven's sakes, you don't have to knock. The door is open.
Just come in," she says. She shifts the papers she has in front of
her to one side and moves her reading glasses to the top of her
head. "So, what is it?"*

*"I've got the design ready for the Marcus account to present
tomorrow."*

*"Just drop it there." She points to a box on her desk. "I'll let you
know what I think later." She returns to the papers on her desk.
Peter recognizes this as a dismissal.*

*Later, at his cubicle alongside his co-workers, Peter sees Angie
approaching. Her deep frown and pinched lips portend trouble.
Peter's heartbeat quickens.*

"Can't you do anything right? This is the worst piece of crap I've ever laid eyes on. I thought you were a creative genius. Ha! Give me a break. My third-grader could do better than this." She tosses the file on Peter's desk. *"I guess we may as well kiss the Marcus account goodbye."* She turns and walks away, not giving Peter a chance to respond. The other employees look away, embarrassed.

APPLYING THE SAY IT JUST RIGHT MODEL

DECISION POINTS

Peter defines the cost. He's been in the department for four and a half months. Each time he submits a design to Angie, she berates him and his work. With no knowledge about what the client wants, she, nonetheless, refuses to listen to his ideas and belittles anything he suggests. He goes home frustrated. He's lost many a night's sleep worrying over Angie and her response to his work. Is her negative treatment worth it? He knows he's talented and can find a job someplace else. On the other hand, he loves his job. He likes the autonomy. He works directly with clients and can expand his creative talent because he works on a broad range of accounts. He likes the other people in his office. If it were not for Angie, he'd be very happy. Because Angie is demanding and intimidating with everyone, he realizes he is working with a *Difficult Person*.

Peter sets the limits. Peter admits that Angie has a lot of experience. Furthermore, her creative talent astounds him. Unfortunately, he cannot brainstorm ideas with her because she demeans everything he suggests. He decides that he will no longer take her verbal abuse. If she has ideas and suggestions for his designs, he will listen but only if she presents them as honest, constructive feedback and not with abuse. If she continues to abuse him verbally, he will polish up his portfolio and begin searching for a job elsewhere.

Peter looks at the power sources. Peter has allowed Angie to believe she's in the seat of power. She thinks she can kick him, yell at him, abuse him, and he will take it. He recognizes that his inability to reassert his position adds to the problem. Peter knows people respect Angie for her creativity but not for her people skills. Recent rumors suggest members of the board worry about how many talented people have left her department. If he resigns after less than five months, it will not bode well for Angie. He sees that he has more power than he realizes.

PERSONALITY OVERLAY

Peter looks at Angie's behavior to determine her personality type. He rules out Sympathetic because she has trouble listening, and compassion is not one of her strengths. He does not see her as an Expressive because she does not spend time talking with anyone. Furthermore, as far as he can see, she has no friends. He suspects that she is either a Technical or a Bold. She demonstrates characteristics of both styles. She is cautious and detailed about her work. Some call her a perfectionist. She must have the final say on everything that goes out of the department. These characteristics typify a Technical. Her Bold tendencies come across because she acts annoyed whenever he interrupts her, and she talks in quick, short sentences. Knowing he's dealing with a Technical/Bold personality, Peter can adjust his style accordingly.

SAY IT JUST RIGHT CONVERSATION

Peter approaches Angie's office. "Do you have a minute?" he asks. "I'd like to talk about the Marcus design."

Angie moves away from her computer screen and expels a deep sigh. "What's there to talk about? It's all wrong, and we don't have time to redo it."

Peter sits across from her. "It would really help if you could spend a little time with me and tell me what exactly you find wrong with the design." **(Specifies the problem.)**

"Everything is wrong," she says. "They won't buy it the way it is."

Peter persists. "Could you be a bit more specific with me? Even if I don't have time to correct this account, I'd like to know what you are thinking for my future work." **(Invites her to talk.)**

Angie picks up the design and shoves it across at him. "Look at those colors. They're too bright. Don't you know how conservative Marcus is? He'll never go for orange and yellow. You should have realized that when you talked to him."

Peter makes a note on his pad. "Angie, I spent a lot of time talking to Marcus and his VP of marketing. They want to change their direction to mirror the new generation of buyer. We talked about an entirely new look."

She harrumphs. "An entirely new look is one thing; a revolutionary look is another. They'll lose the old buyers."

"So you're saying I went too far?"

"God, how many times do I have to tell you? This is not their thing."

"Okay. I hear what you are saying. It frustrates me that you seem impatient and annoyed when I'm simply trying to understand your suggestions. I feel as if you don't want to share ideas with me. I respect and appreciate your thoughts about how we can get them to stretch without going too far. If we could share ideas—both accept each other's without undue criticism—in a brainstorming mode, it would really help me. Would you be willing to do that?" (**Redefines the problem and joins feelings with fact.**)

Angie takes out a pencil. "If you change this to a square instead of all these circles and if you mute the colors, you might have something. I'd also change the slogan. The one you have is too aggressive for Marcus. Maybe something like . . . "

For the next 10 minutes Angie and Peter brainstorm together. As he listens to her and asserts his own thoughts, she softens.

"Angie, this is great. I really like what you've suggested. I'm going to make the changes tonight."

She scowls at him. "There's no way you can get this ready in time."

Peter says, "Oh yes I can. Even if I have to stay here all night and all day tomorrow, it'll be ready. Thanks for your input."

Before Peter leaves, he says to her. "Angie, I respect your creative mind. But, it's very hard working here when you belittle everything I do. Granted, I haven't worked with Marcus as long as you have so it really helped me to see what you thought would fly and what would not. I think together we came up with a dynamite design that they will go for. Next time I have a project like this, I'd like to get your honest, open feedback—like we just did, only sooner. Would you be willing to do that?" (**Resolving the issue.**)

"What do you mean by sooner?"

Peter knows Angie does not like meetings and will not sit in on client meetings. "After I meet with the client the first time and work up the preliminary designs, I'd like for us to meet for no more than, say, thirty minutes."

"If you think that would help, of course I'll do it. But, e-mail your prelims first to give me some lead time."

He smiles. "Great, no problem. I really like this job and what I'm learning by working with you. I can gain a lot from you if you'll show me just a bit more patience. I cannot learn when you tell me it's all wrong without specifying what is wrong. I want to avoid a crisis like this again."

Angie agrees she, too, wants to avoid a crisis like this.

ANALYSIS

Peter knows that Angie may not change. But, he has reasserted himself and he did it with curiosity and compassion. Creating the right moment and listening with an open mind to her suggestions helped him relate to her. He also did not enter her office in a defensive mode, he entered in a curious mode.

Specify the Problem. The main problem Peter identified was that Angie did not spend enough time with him at the outset of a project and once she got the design, she refused to specify what was wrong.

Invite the Other Person to Talk. Peter persisted in asking Angie for her input on the particular project in question. He pushed her until she gave him specific feedback.

Join Feeling with Fact. He shared his frustration with her impatience and apparent unwillingness to give him solid, constructive feedback.

Resolve the Issue. Peter suggested meeting sooner, but he knew she'd balk at going to client meetings. Her idea about sending a preliminary e-mail suggested that she bought into the solution. Peter added a positive consequence at the end by saying he wanted to avoid crises like this in the future. He also intimated that he liked working there so long as he could get solid feedback from her. If he could not get such feedback, the job would be less pleasing. Dealing with a Bold personality, Peter knew better than to ask Angie for suggestions to solve the problem. Instead, he threw ideas out and gauged her response.

STICKY SITUATION # 2:
HOW TO STAY COOL WHEN YOU'RE IN THE HOT SEAT

Mark works in sales for a large pharmaceutical company. It's time for his performance review. He has focused all year on increasing his numbers as well as increasing his sales. Last year after an average review, his boss, Richard, told him he needed to improve if he wanted to advance in the company. Mark feels as if he's done everything he can to satisfy Richard. As Mark walks into Richard's office for the annual review, his body tenses and his heartbeat quickens.

APPLYING THE SAY IT JUST RIGHT MODEL

DECISION POINTS

Mark determines the costs. In this company without high marks on performance, there is no way to advance. Mark is in his mid-40s. He perceives his time running out. He must move forward in this job or find another job where he can move forward. He does not feel Richard appreciates his work. Nonetheless, he prefers to remain in this company where the benefits are good and where he's established himself.

Mark sets the limits. Last year Richard gave him a middle of the road review. Mark accepted the assessment, but determined he'd do better. This time he will not accept a mediocre review without knowing exactly what Richard expects of him and how he can increase his rating.

Mark looks at the power source. In Mark's view Richard sits in the power seat. He's the boss, and he divvies up the numbers. Mark's only recourse is to resign under protest or to accept what Richard says. This feeling of powerlessness makes Mark nervous before the review begins. Mark has worked in the company for five years and in Richard's department for two. His sales records exceed the other salespeople on the team. He has proven his success both to Richard's boss and to his outside clients. He decides that Richard can't afford to lose him. Not only would the company lose a good salesman, but Mark's leaving would also reflect badly on Richard.

SAY IT JUST RIGHT CONVERSATION

"Well, here we are again," Richard says. "Have a seat and let's get this over with." Richard looks away, shuffles the papers in front of him and bites his lower lip.

"So, what's the verdict?" Mark asks with a chuckle to release the tension in the room.

"Let's just go through this review item by item, okay?" He scowls. "I gave you a 3 out of 5 in working with others in the company. We talked about this last year, and I don't see any improvement."

"I'm really disappointed because I worked really hard this year. I increased my sales by 15 percent. I had hoped that would reflect on my evaluation. Tell me what I'm not doing so I can make corrections next year." **(Specifies the problem while joining feeling with fact.)**

"We're not talking about your sales numbers. I noted that in the second part of the review. This part of the evaluation deals with other issues. Like I said how you treat others concerns me."

"I'm curious to know what you mean. I'm frustrated because I don't see how I can work with others when I'm on the road so much. I'm a lone salesman, remember? What exactly do you suggest?" **(Invites Richard to talk and continues to join feeling with fact.)**

"That's the problem, Mark. You don't see yourself as part of a team. You see yourself as out there, all by yourself—the Lone Ranger. Yet, everything you do affects others in this department."

"So, you're saying I don't show enough appreciation for others in the department?"

"It's not just appreciation. You trample everyone. Just last week when you ran out of samples, you took Mitch's samples without a blink. What was Mitch supposed to do? He had a major presentation to an important client, and he had no samples to leave with them. That made all of us look bad."

Mark nods. "That was foolish of me. You're right. I wasn't thinking about Mitch. I was annoyed because we didn't have enough samples. Next time, I will requisition more samples before I run out."

"That's a good idea. In fact, all the salesmen should keep better track of the samples. You guys think you can toss them to the wind without a thought."

"Are you also saying I should be more conservative in giving my samples away?"

"Well . . . I don't see a problem there with you. You're pretty good. The other guys are more liberal with their sample distribution. But, you do need to consider others before you snatch samples that are earmarked for someone else."

"Okay. What else can I do to improve my relations with others in the company?"

"You need to spend more time with the support staff. I'm not sure you even know their names," Richard adds.

"Lisa and . . . Janie?"

Richard smiles. "Janice. That's my point. Janice has been here for eight months. I know you're on the road a lot, but they feel as if you don't like them. I explained it's not a question of like. You're just very busy. So, I covered for you. I don't like having to do that."

"What you want me to do is spend more time with Lisa and Janice when I'm in the office. Maybe I could take them for coffee one morning a week?" **(Resolves the issue.)**

"There ya go. That wasn't so hard was it?"

"Anything else?"

"No, that about covers it."

"So I get a 3 this time because of these two shortcomings? I find that a bit harsh. Is everything else really okay?" **(Invites more input.)**

Richard sighs and says, "I'm going to up the rating to a 4. But I expect to see some major changes in your behavior. You're one of our top salesmen. People respect you. It would be nice if you'd show them some equal respect."

"Let's just be sure I'm clear. If I never take someone else's samples and put in requisitions for samples as soon as I'm running low, and secondly if I take Janice and Lisa to coffee once a week, my rating will go up next year." **(Clarifies the resolution.)**

Richard rises and shakes Mark's hand. "I see no reason why not. Just show your office colleagues the same respect you show your clients and you'll be fine."

"Thanks, Richard. It helped when you were more specific with what you wanted. Also, I would appreciate it if you'd tell me before our next review when I'm doing something wrong. I'd like to make a correction sooner. My goal is to get to 5 next year. I'm sure I can do that with your help."

"Sure. I'll do what I can."

Personality Overlay

What personality type was Mark dealing with? Let's look at what mattered to Richard. He was most concerned because Mark stepped on other people and because he was not friendly with the support staff. Meanwhile Mark was one of the company's top salespeople. A Technical or a Bold would not care if Mark did not get along well with others. They would more readily recognize results and bottom lines. Richard is likely a Sympathetic. Richard's reluctance to give Mark bad news also suggests he's a Sympathetic. Sympathetics hate to disappoint others.

Analysis

Specify the Problem. Once Mark heard his performance rating, he asked questions to find out what the problem was. He specified that he had hoped to increase his evaluation. Instead it remained unchanged.

Invite the Other Person to Talk. Mark asked many questions from the orientation of curiosity to learn what he could do to improve. He was looking for specifics from Richard. Once Richard pointed out particular interactions or behaviors that bothered him, Mark took responsibility for those actions without being defensive and moved on.

Join Feeling with Fact. Mark said he was disappointed with the evaluation and frustrated with not knowing what to do. Mark is probably a Bold personality. He shared his feelings with Richard only because he knew Richard was a Sympathetic. He did not dwell on those feelings; instead, he stayed on his agenda, namely, to determine what he needed to do to improve.

Resolve the Issue. In cases where you find yourself in the hot seat, it helps for you to suggest changes. Mark told Richard what specifically he would do and repeated the plan several times. When your behavior needs modifying, you are the best person to say what you will do. Others can make suggestions, but when you show initiative as Mark did, it looks as if you really want to improve. Mark also ended with a positive goal: to increase his score to a 5 by next year. Finally, he solicited help from Richard by asking him for input before the year-end review.

STICKY SITUATION # 3:
YOUR BOSS ASKS YOU TO DO SOMETHING UNETHICAL

Cynthia directs the Information Technology (IT) unit in one of the largest financial institutions in the country. Although she runs a section, she's way down the line as far as management is concerned. After much work on the part of Cynthia and her team, this institution incorporated many technological changes in recent years. The firm management, which consists of presidents and vice presidents high up in the organization, lacked understanding of technology and did not trust it. They feared information leaks. After years of working with them, cajoling them, assuring them of safeguards, and promising never to give out information to outsiders that might compromise the institution, Cynthia won their support and trust.

One late afternoon Cynthia's boss, Steve (who functions many layers beneath the firm management group with whom Cynthia's team works), enters her office.

Steve says, "I'm telling you this first. We are finally ready to launch the customer call center. As you know, Bentley and I have been working on this for months. It will save the bank millions once implemented, and it will be a feather in all our caps. But, we've got to get it out fast to beat the competition and gain the edge."

"Congratulations," Cynthia says. "I know how much you've worked to get this far." She also knows Steve's promotion depends on the success of this system. Bentley, his boss, made that real clear to him.

He barely nods. "I want to get the call center in place before the next performance review and before bonuses go out. That means we need to get cracking. We've only got three months. Think you can do it?"

Cynthia draws in a breath. "What exactly will it entail?"

"First of all we'll have to reset the passwords so the people in the call center will have access to our system. That's step one which I anticipate not taking too much time, right?"

Cynthia sits upright. "You're joking, aren't you?" Steve looks away. "I promised firm management that we'd never allow access to outsiders without their input and approval. That was part of the package they finally bought into. They would never approve opening up the system like this."

Steve closes her office door. "You can't say anything about this to firm management. In fact, I'm ordering you as your superior not to say anything to anyone about this. If we do not reset the passwords, we can't launch the system in three months. I figure we can go in later and apologize. It's always better to ask for forgiveness than permission, right? Firm management is overly paranoid. There won't be any security leaks. Don't worry about that. You've got to trust me. Everything will be fine. Once they see how many dollars we save and the share holders jumping for joy, they'll never think twice about the possible security breaches."

Cynthia felt as if she'd been hit with a cement boulder. "I promised firm management. They trust me. I can't just do this and not tell them. That's exactly what I promised them I would not do. If they found out, I'd be fired for sure."

"Listen, Cynthia, you have no choice. This call center is a done deal. I don't want to talk about it further." He rises to leave. Cynthia gets up, too, not sure what she will do.

APPLYING THE SAY IT JUST RIGHT MODEL

DECISION POINTS

Cynthia determines the costs. Her boss gave her a direct order not to say anything to firm management. If she disobeys this direct order, her boss will have grounds to fire her. If she does what her boss wants, her colleagues in firm management will erupt in fury. They will go for blood—specifically hers. Her ability to work for them will end. Trust will be shattered. Furthermore, she gave her word. She cannot, in good faith, turn her back on her promise. That leaves one option. She must tell her boss she cannot do it. If he decides to dismiss her, she'll leave. She likes her job. She's worked her way up, and it pays well. Getting another job like this, especially after leaving this well-respected institution under murky circumstances, will prove difficult. This could be a career-breaking decision. The costs are high on both sides.

Cynthia sets her limits. Cynthia decides she cannot go back on her word without alerting firm management. She cannot alert firm management without directly defying her boss. She decides she will talk to her boss and make it clear she will not change the passwords without the approval of firm management. If they give their approval, she will gladly comply with his wishes.

Cynthia looks at the power sources. By giving her a direct order, Steve made it clear who is boss. He put her in a position of a lowly subordinate whom he dominates and commands. Cynthia knows, however, that her relationship with firm management gives her some clout. They like her, respect her, and trust her. She could do major damage to her boss's reputation. She might get fired, but the odds are she'll be fired anyway. She realizes she has more power than she thought. She also knows that if she changes the passwords, she'll need to involve the Security Department. Security never acts without a nod from firm management. Her relationship with Security gives her a bit more leverage. She's sure they will back her decision not to proceed without firm management's okay.

PERSONALITY OVERLAY

What personality style is Cynthia dealing with? Steve is certainly not a cautious person. Someone, who says, "It's better to ask forgiveness than permission," enjoys taking risks. That characteristic suggests he's either an Expressive or a Bold, not a Sympathetic who tends to toe the line nor a Technical who is overly cautious. Steve wants to launch the call center quickly, and he wants full credit for it, desiring to get a jump on everyone else out there. He demands that Cynthia say nothing. His fast-acting, competitive style suggests a Bold personality type. An Expressive would be more interested in talking Cynthia into doing what he wants—persuading her—rather than ordering her. Knowing she is dealing with a Bold personality, Cynthia can formulate her SIJR Conversation in a firm but clear manner.

Say It Just Right Conversation

Cynthia goes into Steve's office first thing the next morning. She closes the door and sits down. "I've been thinking about what you asked me to do. I'm very concerned that you put me in a position between what you want and my job with firm management." (**Specifies the problem.**)

Steve pulls at his cuffs and straightens his tie. "Cynthia, you work for me, not firm management. You've known that from the beginning. Even though we are all part of this institution, we are far removed from firm management. Your role is to serve IT, not to serve the whims of upper management."

"I know my role. I also know that I cannot do what you've asked of me. My job depends on building trust so we can incorporate our technology up the line and throughout the company. I'm stunned that you want me to put all that aside." (**Join feeling with fact.**)

"I'm asking you to do your job."

"Listen, Steve. You're not asking me to do my job. You're asking me to betray firm management and go back on my word. I'm curious to learn from you what other options there might be? Surely this is not the only way to launch the call center." (**Invite the other person to talk.**)

Steve shifts in his seat. "It's the only way to do it quickly. We can jump through all the hoops and get firm management on board, but that will take months. I want this done fast."

"Let's look at some other options. Firm management knows about the call center. They approved the concept weeks ago. We can go to them and explain how we have to change the passwords to make the system work. I'll put my best tech people on developing protections so we don't compromise our data. I can get on that immediately. Look, Steve, we might not make your deadline, but if we go this route, we can still get the call center going without jeopardizing either of our careers." (**Resolves the issue.**)

Steve scowls and sighs. "Bentley isn't going to like this."

"It's not Bentley whose neck is on the line. All our reputations could suffer if we handle this incorrectly. Furthermore, the entire call center program might collapse. Bentley would not like that one bit. I know that you and Bentley worked hard and want to see it succeed. But, I also suspect that you wouldn't want to endanger all that work. Alienating firm management is not a good way to launch the new call center. It's in your best interests to bring them along, and I can help with that. What prevents you from going through firm management?" (**Invites further talk from Steve.**)

"I am worried that they are so paranoid with protections that they will never buy into the call center."

Cynthia sighs. "That's always a possibility. I've made some major progress with them, and I think as long as we show them that we can do this without causing leaks in the system, they'll approve a pilot. I'm willing to begin that process if you'll give me the go ahead."

"Fine, but if the whole thing collapses, it's your neck in the noose as well as mine."

Cynthia gets up. "I'd rather go down in an honest fight. I'm willing to take that risk with you. Thanks, Steve."

ANALYSIS

Again, Cynthia does not expect to change Steve. She used her persuasive, logical style to convince him of the risks. Knowing he's a Bold, she realized he had not thought through everything. That gave her an edge. She showed compassion for Steve's desire to launch a project he'd spent months creating. She also chose language that a Bold could understand, namely, "neck on the line," "collapse" of the call center, "honest fight," and "share risks."

Specify the Problem. Cynthia immediately told Steve what troubled her, that is, being put in a position between him and firm management. She also specified that she would not go back on her word with firm management.

Invite the Other Person to Talk. Bolds do not need a lot of invitation to talk. They will tell you what they think. Steve did that. He reiterated his order. Rather than get defensive, Cynthia invited him to consider more options. She showed a genuine curiosity when she asked the question, "What other options are there?"

Join Feeling with Fact. Because she was dealing with a Bold personality, Cynthia did not dwell on her feelings. She said she was "concerned." She showed compassion for Steve's desire to get the call center launched and all the work he'd put into the project. Bolds do not like to talk about feelings. She did not overemphasize how distraught, hurt, and betrayed she felt by Steve's request. She actually downplayed her feelings. She did, however, let Steve know the probable consequences of this rash plan when she said she did not want to jeopardize both their careers. Often Bolds do not take the time to think through all the ramifications of their bold moves.

Resolve the Issue. Cynthia suggested ways to resolve the issue that would keep her integrity intact while she continued to point out the negative consequences with Steve's plan to rush the project. Her willingness at the end to take responsibility if the project failed showed the Bold personality that she would share risks. Bolds do not like to admit it when they are wrong. Cynthia did not push him too hard. Instead she agreed to take risks with him, thanked him, and left.

CONCLUSION

We've examined three sticky situations with difficult bosses. The first boss, Angie, was clearly a Difficult Person who was difficult with everyone at her agency. Peter took a realistic approach with her, recognizing the slim chances that her behavior would change. He worked out a solution whereby he could tolerate her inability to communicate with others, benefit from her creative ideas, and keep him from internalizing her criticism.

The other two bosses, Richard and Steve, were not Difficult People. Instead they found themselves in sticky situations where their subordinates harbored major disagreements with them. In these situations Mark and Cynthia formed their SIJR Conversations from a standpoint of genuine curiosity and compassion rather than anger and defensiveness. They, thereby, increased the likelihood that their bosses' behaviors would change.

The next chapter explores sticky situations with co-workers. When we look at these situations, we must also consider whether we are dealing with Difficult People or people with whom we have a problem. Sometimes difficult co-workers demonstrate the traits of a Difficult Person. These people are more challenging, but by using the SIJR Model, you can *say it just right.*

Chapter 4

Sticky Situations with Co-Workers

As we look at sticky situations with co-workers, the Decision Points take on a very prominent role in the SIJR Model, particularly regarding the power sources. The model stays intact, but the amount of leverage we have in these situations changes. We actually have more power with our bosses than we think. As the pool of qualified professionals shrink, companies strive to retain their talent rather than lose it. During the era of the young Baby Boomer, that phenomenon did not exist. Employers believed that if they lost one talented person, they could always find another.

With co-workers, as we'll see in this chapter, the amount of leverage we have with another person diminishes—we can't fire the person or threaten to leave the job. We must, therefore, remember the first of the Three C's, namely, we cannot change another person's behavior, just our own. Sometimes having the courage to *say it just right* and proving ourselves to be confident communicators shifts the dynamic of the relationship. We gain respect, and that respect discourages others from taking advantage of us.

STICKY SITUATION # 4:
AN IMPOSSIBLE REQUEST

Samantha has worked for a large manufacturing company for five years. Six weeks ago she moved laterally to a new position in another division. Dale replaced her. Previously Dale worked for Samantha, and he excelled in his performance. Since Samantha changed jobs, Dale has contacted her on several occasions to ask for help on different projects. Samantha assisted him because she knew Dale was still learning the job and because she tends to enjoy helping people. Recently, however, Samantha has been consumed with her new job responsibilities. She's been working late trying to learn the ropes and to achieve the goals she and her boss set. This weekend Samantha will leave for a regional meeting. She'll be in and out of the office over the next three weeks.

On Friday, Dale calls. The division chief and his budget team are coming, and Dale must prepare a presentation showcasing past achievements that illustrate the department's needs in the coming months. Dale needs help. "You're the only one who really knows this stuff. I'm afraid if they don't see what's been accomplished, they'll cut our budget. I know you're busy with other priorities, but I really need you on this one."

"How much time do we have to prepare?" Samantha asks.

"The team arrives on Friday; that gives us less than a week."

"What have you pulled together so far?"

Dale tells Samantha he was waiting to talk to her before he began pulling things together. He does have the specifics of the presentation, namely, what kinds of information they expect and the duration.

"I can't guarantee I can do it," Samantha says, "but let me see what they need. If you can e-mail me everything you've got, I'll look at it and call you back to let you know my decision late this afternoon."

Dale sighs. "Thanks! I knew I could count on you. I'll get that stuff pulled together and e-mailed right away."

When Samantha looks over what Dale sends, she realizes she cannot help without sacrificing her situation in her current job. It's time for Dale to act alone. Samantha goes over to Dale's office to discuss the matter.

"Look, Dale, I did pull some things together for you. I made a list of everything that needs to be done, but I can't do any more. I've got too much on my plate right now."

Dale's face turns red. "But, you said you'd help. I was counting on you. Now what am I supposed to do? If this doesn't fly, it's not just my butt on the line."

"You don't have to get so hot," Samantha replies. "I did what I could, and that's more than most people would have done."

"What's that supposed to mean? After all I've done for you in the past, I thought you'd be more of a team player than this."

"I am a team player, and you know that. I've always pulled through for you."

Dale rises. "Not this time. You'd better leave. I've got a lot of work to do."

Feeling angry and frustrated, Samantha leaves.

APPLYING THE SAY IT JUST RIGHT MODEL

DECISION POINTS

Samantha weighs the costs. If Samantha does nothing, she has little to lose. She's been helpful to Dale, and she knows it. If fact, the concept of tough love might work best here. Let Dale sink or swim. He needs to do his job on his own without assistance from Samantha. Conversely, Dale and Samantha have always enjoyed a very good working relationship. Samantha likes his energetic, friendly manner. Furthermore, Dale knows lots of people throughout the company, not just in his department. If he freezes her out, she'll feel it in the lunch room and possibly elsewhere. She'd prefer not to leave things on such a sour note.

Samantha sets her limits. Samantha recognizes that she helped Dale for too long. She should have broken away sooner. She also realizes that by waiting she ended up severing their ties too abruptly. She did not handle the situation well. Furthermore, she gave him the impression she'd help him. She should have told him no immediately. By using the word *we* when she asked about the amount of prep time, she left him with the idea that she'd help. Granted she made some mistakes in her dealings with Dale, but her ultimate goal is for Dale to develop the confidence to do his own job. She will no longer drop everything to help him. She will place a limit on what she will do and what she won't do.

Samantha determines the power sources. Samantha knows that Dale has no real power over her position in the company. She has established her reputation as a smart, capable employee. Dale, too, has proven his ability. Because her company values teamwork, if Dale labels Samantha an unworthy team player, it could jeopardize her standing. Samantha does not worry too much about this problem because of her strong reputation with her immediate supervisors. Even though Dale does not intimidate her, she wants to have a good working relationship with him. She envisions him as someone who might be supervising her someday.

Personality Overlay

What is Dale's personality type? We know he's a friendly, people person. He is also persuasive. Competitive Bolds never ask for help, and logical, organized Technicals learn new jobs in their own systematic way. If he were a Sympathetic, he would have shown compassion for Samantha's situation in her new job. A Sympathetic would have also shown more gratitude for Samantha's previous help. In all likelihood, Dale is an Expressive.

Samantha, on the other hand, is not an Expressive. She wants to maintain a good relationship with Dale. She went out of her way to help him with his new responsibilities. Had Samantha been a Bold, she would have ended the ties with Dale much sooner. A Technical would have left systematic instructions for her predecessor. She demonstrated all the characteristics of a loyal, dedicated friend; that is a Sympathetic.

Say It Just Right Conversation

After Samantha returns from her trip, she goes to Dale's office.

"Do you have a second?"

Dale shrugs. "Only a minute. I've got to run these by Legal. What do you want?"

Samantha settles across from him. "I want to talk about what happened last week before I left town. I did not like the way things ended—"

"What do you mean?" he interrupts. "You said you'd help me, and you didn't. End of story. I managed to pull something off. God knows whether it will fly or not."

"Listen, Dale, I'm disappointed that you act as if I never helped you. I recommended you for this promotion because I thought you could do the job. I know I agreed to help you out last week, but I've been doing that now for almost six weeks. I'm frustrated that you are still calling me." (**Specifies the problem and joins feelings with fact.**)

"Don't worry. I won't bother you anymore."

Samantha sighs. "I should have been more direct early on. That was my fault. I really want you to be successful in your position. I know you've got the talent. I thought I was helping you, but apparently, I wasn't. I was probably making you too dependent on me. Tell me what I can do now to turn this around." (**Takes responsibility for her part in the problem and invites Dale to talk.**)

Dale rubs his hand over his head. Finally he says, "You're right, I've counted on you for too much. I guess you've just always been there."

"So what can we do now?" repeats Samantha

"Well, I feel really good about doing the budget stuff since you guided me through the last cycle. And, I've always been fine with handling the staff. It's those presentations that pop up that freak me out. I'm not comfortable saying what we need or where we're going."

"Tell me how the presentation went. Give me a blow by blow."

Dale leans forward. He tells her he pulled together everything she suggested and developed a PowerPoint slide for each request item. He emphasized what they had accomplished over the last year and where he wanted to take the department over the next six months. "When Dr. Jones asked me how much staff I needed, I froze. I think he was looking for places to cut, and my mind went blank. All I could think of was, 'Don't fire anyone on my team.' I had no idea what I might say, but I sure didn't want to lose anyone. So, I blurted out a number. God knows if it was accurate."

Samantha listens. "You know how many people it takes to do the job around here. I'm sure the number you gave him was right on target."

Dale shrugs. "We'll see. I've heard nothing."

"It's too soon. You won't hear anything for at least another week."

Samantha pauses. "Dale, what can I do to help you feel confident with your presentations? It sounds as if you're doing fine with everything else." (**Begins resolving the issue.**)

"Don't leave me hanging out to dry like you did last week."

"I'm sorry about that. I overreacted because I felt you should know what to do. With my new job responsibilities I can't do as much for you anymore, but I'll gladly do what I can. Nevertheless, it's up to you to do the bulk of the work. I'll just be there to take a look at your final product until you feel comfortable. Okay?" (**Restating her limits.**)

"Why don't you start by looking at what I presented and tell me where I went right or wrong?" Dale suggests.

"Fine. E-mail me what you have. I will be out of town again, starting on Monday. But, I'll look at it over the weekend."

Dale gets up. "Thanks for coming by to talk about this. I didn't like the way things ended either."

Samantha smiles. "Let's start over. This time, I'll be clearer about what I can and cannot do. But you must agree to do most of the work. I can tweak what you've done just to make sure you don't step on any land mines. Suppose I agree to do that for the next two weeks. After that, you're on your own. Trust me. You'll be running this place like a pro in no time. You're already doing the job much better than I did; particularly handling those pesky personnel issues."

"That sounds like a good plan. Let's have coffee when you get back," Dale suggests.

Analysis

When Samantha began the conversation, Dale was angry. After she specified the problem, shared her feelings, and invited him to talk, he began to soften. Her Sympathetic style enabled her to listen to him and to ask him direct questions to get him to open up. Expressives like to talk and to share. She gave him an opportunity to rehash what happened.

Specify the Problem. The actual problem was not the most recent issue; instead it went deeper, namely, Dale's dependency on Samantha. When Samantha took responsibility for that dependency, Dale relaxed. If she had blamed him or accused him of not trying to do the job, she would have made him angrier and more defensive. Often in these kinds of situations we look at the surface problem and react to that, rather than address the deeper issue as Samantha did.

Invite the Other Person to Talk. Again, with an Expressive, she had no trouble getting Dale to talk. Nonetheless, Samantha's willingness to admit responsibility unleashed Dale's true feelings. She apologized for not being clearer about her limits, never once intimating that he should apologize for his insensitivity to her work demands.

Join Feeling with Fact. Samantha said she was disappointed that he was still calling her. She reminded him that she'd recommended him for the job, and she still had confidence in his ability. These comments resonated with Dale.

Resolve the Issue. After Samantha made the limits clear, she asked Dale what would help him. He came up with the resolution—that is, to continue to tweak his presentations. She agreed, but only for two more weeks. After that, she told him he'd be on his own.

Undoubtedly Samantha and Dale must continue to work out their differences. By being honest with one another, however, they began communicating more confidently. For Samantha to empower Dale she must allow him to do his job and not do it for him. By overprotecting and not releasing her job to him, she created an unhealthy dependency. When Samantha finally cut ties, he felt abandoned. The SIJR Conversation produced the first step in building a new relationship of empowerment.

STICKY SITUATION #5:
YOU STABBED ME IN THE BACK

Laura is a buyer for a large retail store. She's the newest buyer on the team. Her boss informed her that after she'd been there for six months, she'd earn the right to compete with the other buyers to go on a fashion excursion in Paris. Laura has never stepped foot outside the U.S. but has dreamed of going to Europe her entire life.

Patricia holds the top buyer spot in the division. Her record exceeds everyone else's. Laura notices that the other buyers freeze out Patricia whenever they can. Patricia, however, assists Laura and seems ready to be Laura's friend. In fact, she transferred one of her top clients, Crawford Williams, to Laura. "If you get CW off and running, you'll win the trip to Paris for sure," she said to Laura.

"But, don't you want to go?" Laura asked.

"Nah, I've been so many times. You go and have fun. I'd much rather see you go than one of those nitwits." She nods toward the other buyers and gives Laura a conspiratorial wink.

Patricia usually eats lunch at her desk, alone. The rest of the buyers never ask her to join them when they exit for lunch or when they take off for Friday afternoon happy hour.

Two days later, their boss calls Patricia into his office. When she returns, she announces to the others that she's going to Paris this year after all. She secured the top place in the office once again. Laura stares at her, stunned. She'd nearly wrapped up the deal with CW and that, combined with her other accounts, gave her a solid lead. What happened?

It does not take Laura long to discover that Patricia had tricked her. She'd lured in an old crony at CW by telling him she had a line to show him that would "blow him away." She'd stolen Laura's notes and followed up on Laura's leads with great care. Then, she told their boss that Laura didn't have what it took to be a top buyer. She explained that she'd helped Laura and still Laura couldn't pull it off. She showed her boss Laura's work, pretending it was hers. The boss ordered Patricia to take over. She sewed up the deal and won the trip.

APPLYING THE SAY IT JUST RIGHT MODEL

DECISION POINTS

Laura determines the costs. Patricia's treachery left Laura at the bottom of the heap. She has lost the respect of her boss. He had hired her with enthusiasm because of her previous buying experience. He appreciated her contacts in the industry and expected great things from her. Patricia undermined that confidence. If Laura does nothing, she allows Patricia to win. Clearly, Patricia is not a person whom Laura can trust. Being at the bottom, Laura has nothing to lose in approaching Patricia directly. As Laura sees it, Patricia can do no more damage to her.

Laura sets her limits. Laura decides she will talk to Patricia in order to regain her integrity. She plans not to corner Patricia by insisting that she admit what she had done or by placing blame. Instead she decides to make it clear to Patricia never to undermine her again.

Laura examines the power sources. As is usually the case with co-workers, both have equal power on paper. Patricia, however, has worked for the store longer and has established herself as a valuable buyer. Laura, being new, has not established her reputation. Nonetheless, she came to this store with a flawless record and high recommendations. If she goes to the boss with the support of the other buyers and explains what happened, he may recognize Patricia's duplicity. Laura feels she can secure help from the other buyers. Surely Laura isn't the first person Patricia stabbed in the back.

Personality Overlay

What is Patricia's personality style? She's not a person with compassion nor does she demonstrate the ability to listen. She is a loner. These characteristics rule out Sympathetic and Expressive. She's extremely competitive. Her competitiveness overshadows everything else, including friendships and relationships. Patricia aims to win at all costs. She is also meticulous and careful. Because of her high level of competitiveness and her ability to charm others, Patricia is likely a Bold with strong Technical tendencies. The Technical in her stops her from dealing with situations head on which a classic Bold might do. She prefers an indirect or passive-aggressive approach which typifies back stabbers.

Laura, on the other hand, prefers the direct approach. Laura trusted Patricia even though she saw that others in the office did not. She gave her the benefit of the doubt. Laura wants to be liked by everyone, including Patricia. Laura demonstrates Expressive tendencies with Sympathetic characteristics. Going into the SIJR Conversation understanding Patricia's high need to win and her Bold/Technical style gives Laura a slight edge.

Say It Just Right Conversation

Laura decides not to join the other buyers when asked to lunch. Instead, she seeks out Patricia, whom she finds eating alone in the break room.

Patricia looks up from a magazine and gazes at Laura with raised eyebrows. Laura pulls out a chair across from Patricia and unwraps a sandwich.

"I thought everyone was gone," Patricia says.

"I decided to stay here because I want to have a word with you." Laura watches Patricia who moves her chair slightly back.

Patricia shrugs. "So?"

Laura looks directly at Patricia. "I was shocked and surprised when I heard that you won the trip to Paris. When I learned how you won the trip, I was angry." (**Joins feelings with fact.**)

"What are you talking about? I won it fair and square. You couldn't come through with the CW account that I handed over to you."

"Patricia, no one can hear us. We're alone. You don't have to pretend in front of me. I know you took my leads and presented my work to CW as if it were yours. What confounds me is why you gave me the account in the first place?" (**Specifies the problem and invites Patricia to talk.**)

Patricia gets up. "I don't have to explain anything to you."

Laura continues to watch her. "Listen, Patricia, no one in the office likes you. You've betrayed everyone just like you have me in one way or another. The only person ignorant of your games is Mr. Jamison. I suspect he might listen, however, if more than one of us goes to him to lodge complaints against you. I hope it won't have to come to that." (**States negative consequences based on power sources.**)

"If you're threatening me, forget it. You don't have a leg to stand on. I'm the number one buyer here, and that's a fact no one can deny."

In a softer voice, Laura says, "I'm not denying that you're good. In fact, I wanted to learn from you. I recognize in you the ability to find just the right thing for every client. In that you are amazing. I am curious, though, what is it that causes you to push everyone away, even someone like me who respected you?" (**Recognizes her talent and reinvites her to talk.**)

Patricia looks away. "I don't really mean to. I wanted you to win the trip at first. I really did. But, when I saw those proposals you had for CW, I realized they'd never want to work with me again. You'd sew up the deal and be their first-choice buyer. I guess I didn't want to lose them as a client."

"Sounds as if you are frightened I'm going to steal the accounts you've worked years to cultivate. Why would I want to do that? I can build my own reputation with clients based on my knowledge and experience. In fact, Patricia, I'm not interested in competing with you. I just wanted to learn from you and do a good enough job to have an opportunity to go to Paris. That's all. I don't want your job or to do anything that would jeopardize your job." (**Shows compassion.**)

Patricia sits back down. She offers one of her brownies to Laura. "Are you going to go to Mr. Jamison?"

Laura takes the brownie. "I will if I have to. But, what I'd rather do is figure out a way for us to work together and not kill one another.

Right now I don't trust you at all. How can we rebuild a working relationship given what's happened?" **(Begins to resolve the issue and invites Patricia to talk.)**

"I really screwed up. I'm sorry."

"That's not enough. Being sorry is fine. But, we've got to figure out what to do. Any ideas?" **(Persists in resolving the issue.)**

Patricia takes a long breath. "Maybe I could go to Mr. Jamison and tell him I want to give you the trip this year since you have never been."

Laura thinks. "I'd rather earn the trip myself. I can wait until next year. But, thanks for the offer, anyway. What other ideas do you have?" **(Rejects simple solutions that do not resolve the issue.)**

"Tell you what. I'll give you back the CW account, and I'll leave it alone. I won't interfere at all."

Laura shakes her head. "How can I be sure of that? I've heard that promise before. I can't risk another incident like we just had. I know you feel threatened by me. We've got to figure out a way to work together where you don't feel as if I'm competing for your accounts."

Patricia sits up. "Here's the deal. I didn't just steal your stuff. I adapted it for CW. I made major changes that Mr. Jamison recognized as my work."

"I'm sure he did see your mark on my ideas. But telling him I'm not up to being a top buyer didn't exactly help me." **(Restates the problem.)**

"What would you have me do now?"

"I want us both to go to Mr. Jamison. I want you to tell him how my ideas sparked your creativity. What I want him to do is put us both on the CW account and allow us to work together. The ideas we present them will be neither mine nor yours. They'll be ours." **(Proposes a resolution.)**

Patricia sighs. "If I do that, can we get past this?"

"It would be a good start."

ANALYSIS

There is no guarantee that Patricia will change her behavior. Laura, on the other hand, made it clear what she wanted in order to resolve this problem. She asked Patricia to really stretch. Her assurances that she was not in competition with Patricia helped win Patricia's agreement. Laura must continue to watch Patricia to make sure she does not do anything to undermine her. If she does, Laura must follow through on her threat to join forces with the other buyers and lodge a complaint with the boss.

Specify the Problem. Laura did not begin with specifying the problem. She knew Patricia would be defensive and angry. She wanted to let her know how she felt before she put the actual behavior on the table. When she did say what the problem was, namely, that Patricia took her leads and presented them as her own, she got Patricia's attention.

Invite the Other Person to Talk. Patricia did not want to participate in the conversation. She got up to leave after Laura invited her to tell her what had happened twice. To keep her in the conversation, Laura had to resort to a negative consequence. If Patricia had left, Laura would have had to take the next step, that is, recruit the other buyers to join her in a complaint against Patricia.

Join Feeling with Fact. Laura told Patricia she was surprised and disappointed. She also used her nonverbal behaviors to show compassion by softening her voice. She listened to Patricia's reason for "stealing" her work without judgment and actually showed compassion by assuring her that she did not want to jeopardize or compete for her job. When Laura took the brownie from Patricia, she showed her she wanted to make peace, not war.

Resolve the Issue. Being a Bold, Patricia jumped on the simplest solutions. She began with a heartfelt apology. This tactic usually works because people accept the apology and go on. Laura, however, refused to take the bait. Instead, she persisted in looking for a resolution. When Patricia offered the second resolution, another quick fix, Laura pushed harder. Finally, Laura offered a resolution that would resolve the immediate issue and would begin the long process of building a trusting relationship between Laura and Patricia.

Sticky Situation # 6:
A Co-Worker You Dislike

Beth teaches 3rd grade at a public elementary school. One of her fellow teachers, Maria, gets on her nerves. Beth likes to keep to herself, doing her job and keeping out of school politics. Maria saddles up to everyone she knows and gossips about students, parents, teachers, and anyone else who crosses her path. Every day Maria probes Beth with personal questions like whether she is married, where her husband works, what she likes to do in her spare time, and so on. Beth responds, but the questions feel intrusive. She and Maria meet in the teachers lounge nearly every day at the same time. Beth dreads these meetings even though they are supposed to be her breaks. Lately she's been losing sleep, wondering if she should change jobs just to get away from Maria.

Applying the Say It Just Right Model

Decision Points

Beth determines the costs. Beth fears saying something to Maria because she does not want to hurt her feelings. She changed her break times, but no matter what she does, she runs into Maria. Beth looks at the personal costs of not saying anything. She's losing sleep. Her body tenses whenever she thinks about taking her break. She looks under the stalls in the bathroom to make sure Maria is not there. Her mind constantly struggles with ways to avoid Maria. On the other hand, Beth looks at the costs of confronting Maria. She may hurt Maria's feelings. If she does, Maria will avoid her. What else could happen if she confronts Maria? If Maria's angry, she may say something negative about Beth to Mrs. Lewis, the principal. Maria and the principal are close friends. Beth decides confronting Maria is worth the risk.

Beth sets her limits. Beth realizes that she cannot be friends with Maria. Their personalities blend like oil and water. She does not mind working with Maria, but she and Maria must keep their relationship strictly professional. She is willing to assist Maria on joint school projects and to help Maria with her students whenever she can. She is not willing to share intimate information about herself or to listen while Maria talks about the personal lives of others.

Beth looks at power sources. Beth worries about Maria's relationship with the principal. When Beth came to work in the school, she heard that Maria and the principal had been friends since college. Beth knows that she cannot come between that friendship. On the other hand, Beth excels as a teacher. Her students love her, and the parents rave about her. She's conscientious about her job. Her performance reviews reflect the quality of her work. She knows how hard it is to find skilled teachers. She imagines that Mrs. Lewis will not want to lose her.

Personality Overlay

Looking at Maria's behavior, we discover a friendly, outgoing person, who seems insensitive to Beth's nonverbal cues. Undoubtedly,

Beth's tension reflected itself either in frowns, crossed arms, sighs, or other signals that flew past Maria's radar. From what we know about Maria she is direct and talkative. She shares information about everyone and everything, including herself. These behaviors typify either an Expressive or a Sympathetic. Technicals love their privacy, preferring to keep to themselves. Bolds are direct and tend to be open, like Maria, but they are not as talkative. Because of Maria's insensitivity to the nonverbal cues, it is likely she's not a Sympathetic but an Expressive with Bold tendencies. As an Expressive/Bold, we can predict that she likes being center stage, she likes being liked by everyone, and she prefers a direct confrontation.

Beth, on the other hand, values her privacy. She concentrates on her job and wishes not to hurt Maria's feelings. She typifies a Technical/Sympathetic.

Say It Just Right Conversation

Beth enters the teacher's lounge where she finds Maria alone. The other teachers have gone back to their classrooms. As soon as Beth walks in, Maria smiles and says, "Wow, I love your new haircut. Who's doing your hair now?"

Beth tells her.

"My husband hates when I change my hair. I had it colored a couple of weeks ago—just put in a few highlights for something different. He about freaked. Didn't your husband have a fit when you got it cut? I bet he did," Maria says.

"Maria, I'm uncomfortable talking about personal things like this. That's something I've been meaning to discuss with you. Ever since I came to work here, you have asked me questions about my husband and if I plan to have kids and what my parents are like. It bothers me to share such personal information. I know it is natural for you, but it's hard for me. I also know you don't mean anything bad by it. It's just your style. My style is different." (**Specifies the problem and joins feelings with fact.**)

Maria's eyes widen. For once she looks as if she doesn't know what to say. "Gosh, I'm sorry. I didn't realize you were so sensitive. I was just trying to be friendly."

"I know you were, and I completely understand. It's just that I want you to understand that those kinds of personal things feel intrusive to me. It's really not about you; it's how I feel. You are an awesome teacher. You have a great rapport with the kids. Whenever I approach you with professional questions, however, the conversation drifts to personal things. Help me understand what that's all about." (**Invites Maria to talk.**)

Maria shrugs. "I like to get to know people. I'm a very curious person. Sometimes I can't help myself. Whenever a new teacher joins our faculty, I want to know all about them. No one has minded before. In fact, many of them appreciate my open friendly questions. It makes them feel welcome."

"So you're saying you do this to make the person feel included as well as to satisfy your need for curiosity?"

"I suppose so. I certainly don't want to make you feel uncomfortable. I didn't mean that."

Beth watches Maria and fears she might cry. "Look. Not everyone is a private person like me. Maybe that's it. I'm probably different. I'm sure a lot of people appreciate your warm welcome." She pauses. "I brought this up because I want to work comfortably with you. I want us to be able meet up in the hall without any tension. How do you think we can do that?" (**Respecifies the problem and looks for resolution.**)

Maria's eyes bubble with tears. "My husband tells me I'm too direct sometimes, too. I don't think you're that different, really. I suppose I need to be more careful. I'm sorry." She sniffles.

"I do want to work with you, especially on the May Day program coming up. You've got so many creative ideas. How do you think we should proceed?" (**Invites her to resolve the problem.**)

Maria takes a breath. "How about you tell me when I ask you something you don't want to talk about. I'll try and stay focused on our work, but it's very hard for me. If I go over the line, maybe you could tell me?"

Beth smiles. "Suppose we devise a little signal. I like to use signals with my kids. How about I use the time-out signal?" She demonstrates for Maria.

"That sounds great. So, if I mess up, I'll know right away."

ANALYSIS

Beth was careful not to come on too strong with Maria. She prefaced the SIJR Conversation by saying that she, herself, might be different from other people. In all likelihood she is not. There is no need to make matters worse by saying no one likes these kinds of intrusive questions. We want to be careful not to use explosive words in sentences like, "These questions are rude or unprofessional," or "I don't like to gossip." Maria was already defensive. Beth used compassion to keep Maria from getting angry. She listened to Maria's justification for her behavior in a nonjudgmental way.

Maria admitted she might not be able to change her behavior. Together the two teachers came up with a method to enable Maria to gauge herself.

Finally, Beth played on Maria's desire to be liked. She let her know what she could do to enable Beth to work with her. Being an Expressive personality, who wants to get along with everyone, Maria responded positively to Beth's gentle criticism.

Specify the Problem. Beth avoided using "you" statements. She pointed out that Maria's style and her style were different. She refrained from being judgmental, but at the same time, she stated clearly what she found uncomfortable.

Invite the Other Person to Talk. Even though it would have been easy for Beth to tell Maria what she wanted, namely, not to ask her personal questions, she listened attentively to Maria's side of the story. By so doing, she learned that Maria knew she sometimes went over the line. She, thereby, managed to engage Maria in the solution.

Join Feeling with Fact. Several times Beth said she was "uncomfortable." She used a neutral feeling word. Furthermore, she pointed out that these feelings jeopardized their ability to work together. She managed to stay focused and share her feelings even though Maria was on the brink of tears. Many of us would have backed off when Maria started to cry. Beth did not.

Resolve the Issue. Beth sought a solution that would work for Maria. As the conversation progressed she realized that Maria would have to change her personality style. To ask someone to change who they are is asking more than most of us can deliver. Beth persisted with Maria until they came up with a mutually acceptable, realistic solution —a signal that made it easy for Maria to recognize Beth's limits in a nonthreatening way.

Conclusion

As we've seen in this chapter sticky situations with co-workers take a lot of forethought. In the first situation, Samantha allowed a bad situation to go on for too long. It nearly ruined a good relationship. In the second situation, Laura attacked the problem with Patricia's deception right away. The third situation showed us another incident where a bad relationship went on so long that Beth considered leaving a very good job to escape it. The Decision Points helped each person recognized what held them back and what they had to lose if they did not confront the problem directly. After analyzing the costs, limits, and power sources, Samantha, Laura, and Beth decided to act. In certain cases, however, we may decide not to act. The Decision Points enable us to explore and analyze this question in order to choose the best course of action.

In the next chapter we examine sticky situations with clients. Because clients pose a unique set of issues, we may run into a sticky situation where our speaker decides not to conduct an SIJR Conversation.

Chapter 5

Sticky Situations with Clients

A customer breaks his word, chews out someone on our staff, or keeps calling us in the middle of the night. What do we do? Do we shrug it off, remembering the customer is always right? When looking at sticky situations with customers, we sometimes decide to put our heads in the sand. Maybe those customers are a bit difficult to work with, but they bring us lots of business, right? Is the business they bring us really worth the trouble? Therein lies the fundamental question. Are valued employees deserting us while we keep our pesky client? Are we losing much-needed sleep while we struggle over what to do about this client? Are we suffering inside because of what a client is putting us through? How much value does this client really bring? Where do we draw the line in the sand?

I wish I could answer these questions. Unfortunately, I can't. We must decide when we've reached our point of saturation. What I can tell you is that we do have permission to fire clients. I suspect many of us think of our customers as rare commodities that we must embrace for dear life. We believe we can't afford to lose a single paying customer. In Michael Port's best-selling book, *Book Yourself Solid*, he says the way to really be successful is to get rid of dead-weight clients.

He challenges his readers to purge their client lists.[1] A psychiatrist colleague of mine tells patients who refuse to put forth the effort to get better, "You're wasting your money and my time." Do we really want to waste our time and energy on people who rebuff the rules?

Some of you, however, cannot purge your clients. Some of you work in the public sector where outsiders mandate that you work with a certain population of people, regardless of how troublesome. You do not have the power to purge; you do have the power to *say it just right*. I will add one caveat for the public sector readers: Document everything you say or do. If you have a difficult client and you approach that person according to the SIJR Model, consider having someone else present during the SIJR Conversation. In reality, none of us takes pleasure in losing clients. We want everyone to like us and to want our products or services. When we have troublesome, untrustworthy, dishonest, or down-right mean clients, however, the SIJR Model can open opportunities to discover a workable solution.

STICKY SITUATION #7:
THE CLIENT WHO DOESN'T PAY YOU

Brooks is a business coach. He's run a psychotherapy practice for about 15 years. During the last 12 months, he began accepting coaching clients. One big difference between a psychotherapy client and a coaching client (besides the fact that the coaching client does not come to Brooks from a broken place, but from a healthy place) is that the coaching client does not have access to third-party payment. All Brooks's psychotherapy clients pay their bills through their insurance companies.

Two months ago, Brooks met Chloe, a young woman who is starting out in business. He met her at a Chamber of Commerce function. She consented to the introductory coaching session in which she agreed to Brooks's fee structure. Chloe struggles with her finances. Right now she is pouring everything she makes back into her new business. She began working with Brooks to dig her way out of the debt she had accumulated over the last year. Chloe responds to Brooks's challenges and meets the goals she sets for herself. A likeable, even-tempered woman, she draws people to her. Brooks knows her business will thrive and will bring a much more promising financial future.

Unfortunately, Chloe has never paid Brooks. They have had eight sessions which, Chloe says, have been very valuable to her. Brooks billed her twice but has not received a single payment.

APPLYING THE SAY IT JUST RIGHT MODEL

DECISION POINTS

Brooks weighs the costs. Chloe has been a reliable client who has made great progress with her goals. He knows that he is helping her. Breaking the relationship feels wrong to Brooks. He recognizes, however, that he does not perform a charity service. Chloe agreed to the fees when she entered into service with Brooks. If he loses her as a client, he loses no income. He merely loses someone who consumes his valuable time.

Brooks sets his limits. Brooks knows that Chloe has been working on her debt and her finances. Her business is just starting to take off. Soon she will feel more robust. He decides that he will talk to her during their next session. As a coach, he plans to help her work out a payment schedule that will begin right away. If she cannot keep to the schedule, he will stop seeing her.

Brooks looks at the power sources. At some point Brooks wants to convert his therapy practice into a coaching practice. Chloe knows many people in the community and would be a good referral partner. If Brooks stops seeing her, she may react with anger and give his new coaching practice a bad reputation. Brooks, however, doubts that Chloe will respond negatively. She admits she has a problem with finances. He suspects that when he makes it clear that she must either pay him or terminate the coaching relationship, she will decide to do what it takes to continue coaching.

PERSONALITY OVERLAY

We notice several things about Chloe's personality. She is reliable, even-natured, and a compliant client about everything except paying her coach. These characteristics suggest a Sympathetic personality. An Expressive would worry too much about not being liked to be delinquent on her bills. She's clearly not a Technical, who would never enter into a contract with someone she couldn't pay. A Bold would have negotiated for a lower fee at the outset.

SAY IT JUST RIGHT CONVERSATION

"Chloe, we have worked together now for two months and I've sent you two invoices. I'm disappointed that you have not paid me for our coaching sessions," Brooks says at the outset of the session. (**Specifies the problem and joins feelings with fact.**)

"I'm really sorry. You know how strapped I've been. I thought I could pay you last time, but then I got that bill for the electricity when the tree hit the power line. That really threw me."

"I'm curious to know how valuable you believe our sessions are?" (**Invites Chloe to talk.**)

"God, you've saved my life. You've really helped me set some important goals and reach them. I appreciate everything I'm learning about myself from our sessions. I anticipate that next month I will finally see a small profit in the business. And, I've reduced my debt by one-third since we've been working together."

"So, clearly you value what we've been doing. I am pleased that I could help you achieve your financial goals. I remain distressed, however, that you have not kept your promise in our coaching agreement. What can you do to turn that around?" (**Looks for resolution.**)

Chloe sighs and thinks. "I can put off paying off one vendor until next month. That way, I can pay you for part of the bill."

"What will you do to pay the rest of the bill?"

"I will have the entire bill paid off by the end of next month."

Brooks takes a breath. "By then we will have had three more sessions. What will you do to make sure you pay all subsequent bills on time while we are working together?"

"I'm sure that I'll be able to pay regularly once the business picks up. This past year has been very tight. Finally, I can see some progress in everything, especially my debt reduction. If you can give me a couple more weeks, I'm sure I can get it all paid."

"It has been a bad year for you. I know that. Starting a new business takes a lot of guts and courage. You've shown you have what it takes. I applaud you for your work and will gladly give you more time within limits." He pauses.

"So, just to be clear," Brooks continues. "You're saying you'll pay part of my bill now and the rest by the end of the month, right? When will I see those results?"

"As soon as we finish this session, I'll make the first payment online."

"Next time, if you can't pay me, all I ask is for you to tell me. We can work out a payment plan if necessary. It's much better to say something than to let the invoices go unpaid. Will you agree to do that?"

"Of course. I'm sorry. I just thought I'd be able to pay and everything would be fine. I'll let you know if something comes up, though, and I can't pay your next invoice."

ANALYSIS

Will Chloe pay the bills? Brooks knows that she's a reliable client in every way except payment. Now that he's talked to her directly about the problem and made his position clear, she sees her choice. She must either pay her bills or lose him as a coach. He did offer to allow her to pay on a payment plan if she tells him she's having trouble. Both Chloe and Brooks are Sympathetics and as such each wants to please the other.

Specify the Problem. Brooks began the session by stating the problem. Had he waited until the end of the session, he would have given her one more "free" coaching opportunity. He not only stated the problem he also told her he was disappointed that she had not complied with their coaching agreement. For a Sympathetic like Chloe, that statement hit hard.

Invite the Other Person to Talk. When Brooks asked Chloe about the value of coaching to her, he gave her an opportunity to talk. While talking, she shared how much Brooks had helped her with her financial problems. She gave him credit for relieving her financial woes. She herself made it clear that she needed to pay him for his work.

Join Feeling with Fact. Once Chloe told Brooks how much coaching had helped her, he reemphasized his feeling of distress that she had not kept her part of the bargain.

Resolve the Issue. As Sympathetics, Chloe and Brooks had to avoid the impulse to apologize to one another and then let the matter rest. Brooks forced himself to continue to ask Chloe how she planned to pay him. When she offered to have the bill paid by the end of the month, he pushed harder to make sure she understood he also wanted payment for current sessions as well. Finally, he insisted that she tell him when she felt strapped. He let her know he'd work with her if she showed the courtesy to advise him.

In the end, if Chloe does not pay Brooks as she promised and if she does not alert him, he will stop coaching her. The SIJR Conversation made that potential outcome clear.

STICKY SITUATION #8:
THE CLIENT CHEWS OUT YOUR STAFF

Dr. Nash runs a medium-sized veterinary clinic that specializes in small animal medicine. His receptionist, Donna, receives high praise from his clients because she's personable, reliable, and loves animals. One morning a longtime client, Mrs. Lane, presented her dog for surgery. As was customary for a 10-year-old dog, Donna asked Mrs. Lane if she wanted to run blood work on him before the surgery. Dr. Nash recommends this procedure for older or at-risk animals in order to take all precautions during surgery. Mrs. Lane said she wanted to run the blood work and to please do whatever was necessary for her dog.

That afternoon Mr. Lane came to pick up the dog. When he looked at the bill, his face turned red, and he shouted at Donna, "What do you people think you're doing charging this much for a routine operation? I never authorized you to run all these ridiculous, add-on tests."

Donna explained that Mrs. Lane signed the forms to run the tests. But, Mr. Lane cursed her and called her a stupid cow, shouting, "My wife has no idea about these things. You know you should contact me. We've been coming here long enough that any idiot, even one as dense as you, would know what to do."

"Mr. Lane, please calm down. I'm sure we can work this out," Donna said. Her voice broke; she was nearing tears.

"I don't ever want you touching my dog again. And, I'll be damned if I'm going to pay this outrageous bill." He stormed out the door with his dog.

Later Donna reported the incident to Dr. Nash.

APPLYING THE SAY IT JUST RIGHT MODEL

DECISION POINTS

Dr. Nash weighs the costs. The Lanes, with their two cats and one dog, have been good clients for the past three years. They bring their animals in for regular exams and purchase products from the clinic. The clinic staff like Mrs. Lane, but they all cringe when Mr. Lane appears. This isn't the first time that he's been angry and belligerent. Dr. Nash feels sorry for Mrs. Lane, who wants to take care of her animals. This time, however, Mr. Lane crossed the line when he became verbally abusive to Donna. Dr. Nash decides that the Lanes's business is not worth it to his clinic. The clinic has developed a good, loyal clientele over the years. Dr. Nash suspects that even if Mr. Lane badmouths his clinic, it will not dissuade others from coming because he knows he's a good veterinarian.

Dr. Nash sets his limits. If clients are dissatisfied with the care an animal gets or with the charges the clinic imposes, the client must talk directly to Dr. Nash. He will not work with clients who scream at his front desk staff or any of his techs.

Dr. Nash determines the power sources. Because he feels confident that his business will not suffer if he loses the Lanes as clients, Dr. Nash sees himself in the seat of power. Even though Mr. Lane is the kind of person who will go out of his way to spread negative information about his clinic, Dr. Nash trusts that people will recognize Mr. Lane for what he is.

PERSONALITY OVERLAY

We can see from Mr. Lane's behavior that he is a Difficult Person. He appears to be difficult with everyone, not just a single person. We also predict that he is not a Sympathetic, who tends to listen and show compassion. In all likelihood Mr. Lane is not an Expressive because Expressives like for other people to like them. That does not mean that Expressives do not lose their tempers, but they tend to do so infrequently. We suspect, therefore, that Mr. Lane could be a Bold or a Technical personality. Bolds are quick to jump to anger and tend not to listen well. Technicals are overly cautious and sometimes believe that others are looking for ways to "rip them off."

Realizing that Mr. Lane is either a Bold or a Technical, Dr. Nash can construct the SIJR Conversation. To compensate for the Bold, he will need to set his limits but without embarrassing Mr. Lane for behaving as he did. The Technical in Mr. Lane will want to understand logically the need for the tests and how Dr. Nash arrived at the charges.

SAY IT JUST RIGHT CONVERSATION

Dr. Nash decides to conduct the conversation by telephone. He reaches Mr. Lane at home the evening after the incident.

"Hello, Mr. Lane. This is Dr. Nash. How is Muffin doing?"

"He's fine. My wife tells me he's eating well and taking his pills."

"I'm glad to hear that. If you have a moment, I want to talk to you about the incident that occurred in the clinic this afternoon. I understand that you were upset because we ran blood work on Muffin before the surgery. What troubled you about that procedure?" **(Invites him to talk right away.)**

"It's not the procedure that bothered me. I was furious because no one asked me. You people think you can run a $100 worth of blood work and get away with it. I'm not going to pay for unnecessary tests."

"So, what you're saying is that you were upset because we did not get your permission before running the tests."

"You got that right. My wife said it was okay, but she's a softy. She'd toss all our money out on these stupid animals if I didn't watch her. Your people know that. You took advantage of her. You should always call me."

"Mr. Lane, we consider you and your wife Muffin's owners. It is common practice for us to ask whoever brings the animal in for permission to run tests. We will gladly put a note in your file, however, if you want us to contact you for all clearances. That's not a problem. But, I must say, I was distressed when I heard the way you spoke to Donna. She was doing her job as I instructed her." **(Specifies the problem.)**

"Yeah, well, I do spout off sometimes. Especially when I think people are taking advantage of me."

"I realize you were angry and probably not yourself. But, I cannot have clients yelling at my front desk staff. Donna is a longtime employee, one of the best. I feel fortunate to have her working for me. What do you think we can do to prevent this from happening in the future?" **(Shows compassion, sets limits, and invites resolution.)**

"First of all, don't touch any of our animals without talking to me."

"That is something we can do. In fact, if you are unhappy with the way our clinic operates, I will be glad to send your files to another vet. That's no problem." **(Sets consequences.)**

"No, I like you and want to keep bringing my animals to you. My wife likes your clinic. I just want to be sure I know how much things are going to cost up front."

"Sometimes we don't always know the exact costs. But, we do try and contact people if there is a procedure that we did not talk to you about. In the future, however, if you have a problem with anything that we do, I prefer for you to talk directly to me." **(Looks for resolution.)**

"That's fine."

"There is one other problem. Donna is very upset. How do you suggest we help her to feel better?"

"That's your problem as I see it."

"I've told her that you were upset and did not mean all the things you said to her. But, I don't want an awkward situation when you or Mrs. Lane return to the clinic. What could we do to make that happen?" (**Invites Mr. Lane to resolve the issue.**)

A long silence ensues. "I suppose I could tell her I'm sorry I yelled at her and next time I'll yell at you instead." He laughs.

"Let's try and refrain from all the yelling. Things work out much better for everyone when we can stay calm. But, I would appreciate your apologizing to Donna. Meantime, I will put a note in your record to contact you for all decisions related to your animals." (**Summarizes the resolution.**)

"I'm not going to pay for those tests."

"We customarily recommend running blood work on older animals, but I will take those charges off Muffin's invoice this time. If, however, you are upset in the future and you display that to my staff, I will have to ask you to find another vet. My staff is too important to me." (**Restates the consequences.**)

"Sure, I'll come to you if I have any problems or questions."

ANALYSIS

Dr. Nash used nonexplosive words to keep Mr. Lane calm (words like distressed, rather than outraged or angry). At the same time, he set clear limits. Dr. Nash showed great patience as he listened to Mr. Lane. He suggested he find another vet, but Mr. Lane wanted to continue using Dr. Nash's clinic. Whether or not Mr. Lane changes his behavior is a toss up, but Dr. Nash made the consequences clear: Yell at my staff and you'll have to find another vet.

Specify the Problem. Dr. Nash did not immediately jump right into the problem. Instead he began by asking questions to find out from Mr. Lane what happened. Often in these situations, we jump right in without giving the other person a chance to tell his or her story. By allowing Mr. Lane to vent and share his concerns, Dr. Nash softened him before getting to the actual problem.

Invite the Other Person to Talk. Dr. Nash invited Mr. Lane to talk immediately and continued to do so throughout the conversation. At the end, he wanted Mr. Lane to apologize to Donna, but he wanted him to come up with the idea. If Dr. Nash had made the suggestion, he would have lessened the likelihood of it happening.

Join Feeling with Fact. Dr. Nash joined feeling with fact throughout the conversation. He began by saying he was distressed. He asked Mr. Lane to talk about his feelings and how to resolve the issues that sparked those feelings.

Resolve the Issue. Dr. Nash's overlying issue was to stop Mr. Lane from chewing out his staff. He, therefore, agreed to Mr. Lane's desire to make the decisions for the animals, and he also agreed to adjust Mr. Lane's bill. In return Mr. Lane must bring his concerns to Dr. Nash, rather than yell at the front desk staff, and he must apologize to Donna. If Mr. Lane does not comply, Dr. Nash made the consequences clear.

FIRING THE CLIENT

Some of you may wonder why Dr. Nash didn't simply fire the obnoxious Mr. Lane. After all, Dr. Nash's success did not depend on the Lanes' business. Had Dr. Nash applied the Decision Points and realized that firing the client was the best option, he would have proceeded with that intention as noted below.

APPLYING THE SAY IT JUST RIGHT MODEL

Dr. Nash wants to avoid missteps when firing a client like Mr. Lane. If he uses explosive words with a highly charged Bold, he might find himself in a dangerous place. The goal here is to let the client know that he is no longer welcome in the clinic without incurring too much wrath.

When firing a client, you can still use compassion and you may want to show curiosity. One caution, however, if you show too much curiosity the client might believe he or she can remain your client. If you clearly want to end the client's business, it's best to state the problem and to move to the next steps without too much conversation.

SIJR CONVERSATION TO FIRE THE CLIENT

Dr. Nash chooses to telephone Mr. Lane at his home the evening of the incident.

"Hello, Mr. Lane. This is Dr. Nash. How is Muffin doing?"

"He's doing fine. My wife tells me he's eating and taking his medication."

"I'm glad to hear that. I wanted to talk to you about the incident that occurred in the clinic this afternoon. I am a person who treasures the work my staff do. It troubled me the way you spoke to Donna. To resolve the issue, I'm canceling your bill. You do not need to pay for the services rendered today. But, we will no longer be treating your animals. When you've found another vet, we will gladly send our records to that clinic."

"So, you don't want our business?"

"I'm willing to give up your business for the sake of harmony among my staff. I like your animals and have enjoyed treating them. If, of course, Muffin has any complications from today's procedure, I will take care of him. Meantime, let me know when you secure another vet."

ANALYSIS

This time Dr. Nash did not invite Mr. Lane to talk. He specified the problem and joined feelings with facts. Rather than invite Mr. Lane to talk or invite him to help with resolving the issue, Dr. Nash ended the conversation by stating the next steps. He did not give Mr. Lane an opportunity to share his story or to help come up with a mutual decision.

There is nothing wrong with deciding to fire a client if that client's behavior disrupts the harmony of your business or threatens you or your staff. It is important, however, to go through the Decision Points to make sure you've considered every angle and narrowed down that firing the client is the best option.

STICKY SITUATION #9:
A CUSTOMER WANTS A KICKBACK

Anthony runs a very successful restaurant called Mangia. He created a new type of fast-food dining in which his cooks prepare everything in an open, clean kitchen. The guests order their type of pasta and their choice of sauce. The menu is limited, but Anthony prides himself on serving the freshest food he can find. One of his vendors, Martin, delivers fresh vegetables daily and has done so since Anthony opened the restaurant five years ago. They have a very good working relationship. Recently Martin's son, Pete, took over Martin's business. Pete continues to deliver fresh products to Anthony on time each day. During his last delivery Pete drew Anthony aside and said, "I want to talk to you about a deal I'm putting together."

"Sure."

"I've got some people with deep pockets. They would be willing to pay for you to franchise this place. I told them all about you and what you do here. They are anxious to talk to you. One said we could get this idea franchised and probably make millions. We could be the McDonalds of Italian eating."

Intrigued and excited by the idea, Anthony agreed to meet Pete's friends. They arranged a time and a place to get together.

"By the way," Pete said to Anthony before he left, "If they bite, I want a cut. I'm thinking about a $10,000 finder's fee and some portion of the profits. That's only fair."

Anthony, too surprised to say anything, simply mumbled something about talking about that later.

Applying the Say It Just Right Model

Decision Points

Anthony determines the costs. Anthony knows that his restaurant could be franchised. He'd thought about pursuing that opportunity in the past but didn't know where to begin. Pete opened a door. But, he feels very uncomfortable with Pete's proposition. Even if he pays him the "finder's fee," the fact that he wants a cut in the profits sounds either unethical or exorbitant to Anthony. If he franchised his business name and his business idea, he should not have to share profits with someone who has had so little to do with his success. Anthony has two worries. One, if he does not pursue Pete's lead, he may lose the opportunity to franchise. Two, if Pete gets angry with him, he may terminate their business relationship. It would be hard for Anthony to find a vendor of similar quality and reliability.

Anthony sets his limits. Anthony would be willing to pay Pete for connecting him to these people. The fee Pete suggested sounded too steep to Anthony, but he'd be willing to negotiate this. He, of course, would not want to pay the fee if the deal fell through. After much thought, Anthony decides he will not dish over part of his profits to Pete unless Pete agrees to contribute financially to the creation of the new stores.

Anthony determines the power sources. From Anthony's point of view, Pete has the power. He knows the people willing to pay for a franchise. Undoubtedly if Anthony turns down the opportunity, Pete will find someone else for these unknown people to franchise. When Anthony thinks about it, however, he recognizes that few people offer as high a quality a product as his. Indeed, the appeal Pete offers to the investors is Anthony and his business. If Anthony turns Pete down, Anthony, himself, could find others willing to put up money for a franchise.

PERSONALITY OVERLAY

In all likelihood Pete is not a Technical whose cautious personality would never lead him to a venture as risky as a franchise. Pete is probably not a Sympathetic because a Sympathetic would naturally help someone out, without asking for a "finder's fee." Pete, therefore, is likely either a Bold or an Expressive. We know he is a people connector and a persuader. Such characteristics typify an Expressive personality. He definitely has Bold characteristics as well because Bolds never shy away from risk and would naturally ask for a kickback.

Knowing that Pete is likely an Expressive/Bold enables Anthony to plan his SIJR Conversation in order to create an atmosphere of negotiation.

SAY IT JUST RIGHT CONVERSATION

Anthony decides to go see Pete the next day.

"Pete, let's talk some more about the proposition you brought to me yesterday. I must say, you took me by surprise. I'd like to learn more about what you have in mind." **(Invites Pete to talk.)**

"Sure thing. I talked to these guys, like I told you. They have really deep pockets and are interested in investing in some kind of restaurant venture. I told them about you and how my dad has worked with you for so long and trusts and respects you. They were intrigued by the simplicity of your operation. Anyway, they want to talk and asked me to put together a meeting. At this point they just want to meet you. I don't think you need to worry about making a presentation or anything."

"Why don't they just come have a meal at Mangia's instead of us meeting someplace else? That way they can see what the restaurant is like."

"Good idea. I'll give them a call right now."

"Wait one minute. I have something else I want to talk about. You mentioned a finder's fee and a cut in the profits. I have to tell you that arrangement really bothers me. I was disappointed that you felt like you needed to be paid to help me out. Your dad and I always did business man-to-man because of our respect for one another." (**Specifies the problem and joins feeling with fact.**)

"Oh gosh, I respect you. Don't get me wrong. But, I see this as a huge opportunity, and I wanted to have some piece of it. That's all. It's not a question of respect."

"In that case, we need to talk about what is fair. I will pay you a finder's fee if the deal goes through, but I'd like to talk about a couple of restrictions. First, if you want a percentage of profits, you must contribute to the costs I will incur with the growth. In that case, I see no point in a finder's fee. If you want to become my exclusive vendor, then, again, I see no point in the finder's fee. I will pay the fee if you do not want to continue our relationship, of course." (**Sets limits and specifies consequences.**)

"Hold on! I want to continue providing our products to Mangia. Naturally, if you expand your orders, it will help us, there's no question about that. I can see where you are coming from about the fee. So, if the deal goes through, and we do not have an exclusive relationship or some sort of profits deal, but we have an informal relationship as we now have, you'll pay the fee?"

"That's right."

"Hum. Let me think a minute."

"If we share profits, then you have to take the same financial risks I take. What do you think?" (**Clarifies limits and invites Pete to talk.**)

"Maybe the best thing for us would be a finder's fee outright. If you expand your orders, we will increase our profits accordingly. Maybe after you get going, we can talk about developing an exclusive relationship. We are not ready for that now because we have other clients who depend on us." (**Resolves the issue.**)

"That's what I thought. Okay, if the deal goes through, I will pay the fee, but $10,000 seems steep to me."

Pete laughs. "That's because you haven't talked to my guys. When you do, it will seem like small potatoes. They've got big ideas."

"Because I've known your dad for so long, I'm going to put my trust in you. If what you say is true and the deal goes through, I'll pay you $10,000."

"You won't be disappointed."

ANALYSIS

Anthony came into the conversation with a clear idea of what he wanted. He did not jump into resolving the issue. Instead, he set his limits and then encouraged Pete to think about what he said from a business standpoint. Pete came up with the resolution on his own.

Specify the Problem. After Anthony invited Pete to talk, he clearly said what troubled him, namely, the finder's fee and Pete's desire to have a cut in the profits. He couched these concerns in terms of mutual respect. Because Pete is an Expressive, he responded quickly to the respect issue.

Invite the Other Person to Talk. Anthony invited Pete to talk right away, but not about the specific problem. Instead, he warmed him up by getting clarification on the meeting agenda. He almost lost Pete when Pete offered to telephone his contacts immediately. Anthony was quick to bring him back by stating the problem. Later, Anthony invited Pete to talk more by asking him to respond to the limits he set.

Join Feelings with Fact. Anthony *said it just right* when he spoke about "respect" regarding his relationship with Pete's father. He mentioned this mutual respect early in the conversation and then at the end of the conversation. In both instances he was letting Pete know that their businesses were deeply rooted in longtime trusting relationships built by his dad.

Resolve the Issue. Anthony allowed Pete to come up with the decision neither to be a partner nor to have an exclusive vendor relationship. He put the matter before Pete in an honest and open way. Pete realized that sharing profits when he was taking no risks was not fair to Anthony and something Anthony would not accept. He quickly acquiesced to Anthony's terms. By showing a willingness to pay the fee, Anthony proved to Pete that he trusted him.

CONCLUSION

We've looked at three kinds of sticky situations with clients. In the first situation where the client did not pay for the services rendered, Brooks had to firmly specify consequences. In the second situation where the client chewed out a valued staff member, we saw that Dr. Nash had two options: One, to set clear limits and continue to work with the client, or two to fire the client. In the third situation we saw a client/vendor who wanted a kickback for services rendered. In this situation Anthony set clear limits, stated what he wanted, and showed a willingness to negotiate.

As we saw in Chapter 3, many workplace sticky situations occur between bosses and subordinates. The next chapter examines how to apply the SIJR Model when facing a disciplinary conversation or when bosses have to deliver bad news.

NOTE

1. Michael Port, *Book Yourself Solid* (Hoboken, NJ: John Wiley & Sons, 2006).

Chapter 6

Sticky Situations with Subordinates

A Gallup report says, "Employees don't leave jobs, they leave managers."[1] The Gallup organization learned this fact after four decades of research and surveys of workers in all kinds of industry. Brad Gilbreath in an article in *Work & Stress* discovered that bosses make a significant contribution to employee stress. He confirmed the Gallup research with a sample of 167 men and women from different kinds of organizations.[2] If you have a bad, frustrating boss, you leave your job even if it is a good job. With the costs for hiring and training new people soaring each year, organizations are looking for ways to retain employees. They pay people like Gallup to tell them what factors keep people happy enough to stay in their jobs.

Daniel Goleman et al. came up with a catchy concept called Emotional Intelligence based on an emotional quotient, or EQ.[3] He discovered that managers with a high retention rate also have a high EQ, meaning they score high on compassion, on listening, and on caring about others. In fact, if you think back on the managers you've worked for in your life, what characteristics did they have? Here are a few I recall: good listeners, positive attitude about my work, challenged me but not beyond my limits, supportive, and enthusiastic.

Goleman found that managers who understood feelings and emotions became more successful leaders. A high EQ score means you are a manager who strives to learn more about yourself and your behaviors in order to improve your skills as a person, not just as a leader. In essence, you learn to care about yourself and about others at the same time.

The Arbinger Institute confirms this insight in its book *Leadership and Self-Deception: Getting Out of the Box*. The authors discuss treating people as people and not as objects. The book helps leaders recognize when they lead from the inside out, that is, inside the box, rather than leading from the outside in or outside the box.[4] Leaders who lead from inside the box have low EQ scores and are blind to how their actions affect others.

This chapter explores two types of sticky situations with subordinates. The first examines a disciplinary situation. The second looks at how to tell someone something they do not want to hear.

How to Discipline Using the SIJR Model

Given what Gallup and Gilbreath learned about leaders and what Daniel Goleman and the Arbinger Institute tell us about Emotional Intelligence, how can those of us who want to be good managers effectively discipline employees?

Discipline carries a negative connotation fraught with memories of trips to the principal's office or of scolding words from our parents. An empathetic manager with a high EQ score might find disciplining tough. In answer to the question—how can we manage with compassion and still discipline—we must understand exactly what discipline means. The word discipline comes from the Latin word *diciplina*, meaning disciple. Wikipedia tells us that discipline has as its root *discere* "to learn," and derives from *discipulus*, or pupil. A disciple, therefore, is a follower or a student. Similarly, to discipline someone means to teach that person. The early 1990s brought a plethora of literature about discipline without punishment in an effort to show that discipline and punishment do not necessarily go together. In fact, while disciplining, a good manager learns to communicate expected behaviors in an open, clear, and direct manner. To discipline, you must employ the principles of the SIJR Conversation; namely, you want to create a two-way dialogue about what you expect and what is possible from both the manager's and the employee's perspective. Coming from an orientation of the Three C's—change, compassion, and curiosity—managers with high EQ scores excel as disciplinarians.

Factors Inherent in Any Disciplinary Conversation

State Behaviors That Must Change. When we specify behaviors in the SIJR Conversation, we identify the behaviors in a way that clearly communicates what we are talking about.

Example: "Sheila, you are turning in your quarterly reports later and later. We did not receive this period's report until two days after the final deadline. I cannot turn in the entire team's numbers until I get your data. It's embarrassing to me when every quarter ours is the last report submitted. I must have your report by the fifteenth of the month and no later."

This example provides Sheila with information about what behavior her boss expects as well as what problems her behavior caused up the line.

Keep the Other Person in Mind. Stone et al., in *Difficult Conversations: How to Discuss What Matter's Most*, talk about telling your story as well as listening to the other person's story. In a disciplinary conversation, we open our minds to the possibility of what the authors refer to as the third story.[5] Your organization may have rules that may no longer prove productive. When you allow employees to share their frustrations, you open up the possibility to the existence of administrative barriers that block productivity.

Select the Right Time and Place. We all remember our dread when our teachers sent us to the principal's office. As children, we recognized the principal's office as a place of power where we did not belong. Before delivering the bad news, think about the place and the time. Find a place that feels safe to the other person. If you work in the world of cubicles, go to one of the conference rooms.

Be careful not to share bad news when the person is experiencing a personal crisis or about to give an important presentation. Select a time that will enable you to have an open dialogue. If the time you select adds pressure, the dialogue will shut down.

Stress Positive Consequences. Often when dealing with performance issues, we think only in the negative. Our challenge is to come up with positive consequences. The behavioral psychologists tell us that mice respond to shocks, but they also tell us mice respond to bits of food. Positive consequences create a willingness to change.

Negative consequences produce a short-term willingness to change only when the axe is hanging over our heads.

Example: "Sheila, if you would get your report to me by the fifteenth, I can complete the team stats in time for us to win the competition. If we win this quarter, our stats will appear in the company newsletter. That recognition might be the boost you've been looking for to get your promotion."

This case is adapted from one that appears in *Difficult Conversations*[6]

Boss: "I wanted to talk to you about my presentation for Client X. You packed the wrong storyboards. The situation was unbelievably awkward and made me look like a fool. We simply can't work this way."

Assistant: "I heard about that incident. I'm very sorry. I just, well, you probably don't want to hear my excuses."

Boss: "I don't understand how you could have let this happen. I trust you to do your job, and now I don't know what to think."

Assistant: "I am *really* sorry."

Boss: "I know you didn't do it on purpose, and I know you feel badly, but I don't want this to happen again, ever. You understand what I'm saying?"

Assistant: "It won't happen again. I promise you."

In this situation the boss is "assuming" he is right and the assistant is the one to *blame* for what went wrong. He is also assuming that it won't happen again. What do you think? Neither person has tried to discover what really happened.

Let's try rewriting the situation above. This time we will try not to assume who is right or wrong, and we will avoid placing blame.

Boss: "We need to talk about what happened when I made the presentation to Client X."

Assistant: "I heard about that incident. I'm really sorry about what happened."

Boss: "As you can imagine, I was very embarrassed to be there with the wrong storyboards. What went wrong?"

Assistant: "I think you earmarked the wrong presentation for that client. I usually recheck because with so much going on, we all get confused. But, you and Jeff and Rita were going to different places on the same day, and I didn't get a chance to do the recheck."

Boss: "Are you saying, I put the wrong attachment to my e-mail to you?"

Assistant: "This has happened before. We all are overloaded. But, I usually double-check."

Boss: "How can we prevent this from happening in the future? I don't want to be caught like that again."

Assistant: "Maybe we can work on the schedule. It helps if we don't have more than two major presentations leaving on the same day. A slight adjustment would have helped all of us."

Boss: "That's a great idea. I'll bring it up at the next team meeting."

As Stone et al. suggest, when the boss and the assistant listen to one another without placing blame, they learn more about what caused the problem and can look objectively for a solution.

STICKY SITUATION #10:
DISCIPLINING THE BOSS'S DAUGHTER

Ivan manages an architectural team, which includes two other architects, Mac and Lois, and one assistant, Emily. The company designs retail structures often for local governments. Mac and Lois have strengths that complement each other, and they work well together. Lois has a bent toward keeping the project environmentally sound while Mac's strengths lie in utility and contemporary design. Emily's job is to support the team. She takes the plans to the production department, and she does some of the lettering. Emily complains that her job is boring. She often forgets to pick up plans or to complete the necessary paperwork to make deliveries. She rarely comes to work on time, and her lunch hours stretch longer and longer each day. More often than not, Ivan catches her on personal calls or texting her friends during the workday. Ivan has spoken to her about these problems, but she shrugs and says, "I'm just bored. Why shouldn't I talk to my friends when I want? There's not enough work here to keep me busy."

Unfortunately, Emily is correct. Ivan hired her under duress. Emily is the youngest daughter of the firm's owner, Mr. Whippet. Whippet asked Ivan to give Emily something to do. At the time Ivan needed a part-time gofer, someone who could run the errands for the team. In the past he hired students from the nearby college. Whippet explained to Ivan he wanted Emily to work full time, and he confidently stated, "I'm sure she can do the gofer's job."

One of Ivan's biggest problems is that Emily's behavior is causing a rift within the team. His otherwise smooth-functioning workers are showing signs of frustration. Mac and Lois snap at each other and argue over designs. Because they have to wait hours on plans that are overdue in production, they are both irritable, not with each other, but with Emily. When Emily finally brings the plans, they have to work long and late hours to get the project completed on time. Mac and Lois know Emily is Mr. Whippet's daughter, and they realize that Ivan's options are limited. Ivan suspects that their tolerance is running out, and he fears one or both will decide to leave the company.

Applying the Say It Just Right Model

Decision Points

Ivan determines the costs. Mr. Whippet made it clear to Ivan that he could not fire Emily. When Ivan told Mr. Whippet that he needed a part-time intern to run errands for the team, Mr. Whippet said, "My daughter would be perfect." Ivan told him he would prefer a student. But Mr. Whippet said, "My daughter is better than a student because she's smart and capable. This would be a chance for her to learn the business. I'm counting on you to mentor her. She is young, though, Ivan. You'll need to bring her along slowly, but I have confidence you can do it." Ivan asked him, "What if it doesn't work out?" Mr. Whippet said, "Well, it just better, right?" He laughed and patted Ivan on the back. The implication was clear.

If Ivan fires Emily, he may very well lose his job. On the other hand, if he does not do something about her performance, he may lose one or two valuable employees. Ivan decides that for the sake of the team, he has to show some leadership.

Ivan sets his limits. Ivan decides that Emily must come to work on time, and she must get the tasks done on time. He cannot have her going off on long lunch hours and returning with the plans late in the afternoon. He does not mind her talking on the telephone or texting her friends *if* she has completed her job tasks. If she does not comply with these requirements, he will report her abuses to her father and request that he reassign her.

Ivan considers the power sources. From Ivan's point of view, Emily has all the power. She knows that her father owns the company, and she knows that her father forced Ivan to hire her. She thinks she can do whatever she wants while Ivan's hands are tied. In fact, Ivan feels so trapped over this Emily problem, he has begun talking to other architectural firms. Unfortunately, at his level jobs are scarce. He'd have to take a significant cut in salary if he changed firms. Mr. Whippet respects his work, however. He's been with the firm for seven years and has won a number of prestigious competitions. Replacing Ivan would not be easy for Mr. Whippet.

PERSONALITY OVERLAY

Ivan knows he is a Technical personality type. He likes things done in a logical and orderly manner. Lois and Mac are less technical, but have learned to work with Ivan's obsessive desire to meet deadlines and to keep to a timeline. Emily, on the other hand, is oblivious to deadlines. She marches to her own drum. Her Expressive personality puts her in contact with many people, usually her personal friends. She has a winning personality, but she also has trouble listening to other's needs. She tends to respond well when praised. Ivan cannot praise her, however, when her work suffers. Emily ignores his suggestions for improvement and seems hurt when he criticizes her. She takes everything he says personally.

Respecting Emily's desire to be appreciated and liked, Ivan can now more logically apply the SIJR Model and conduct a disciplinary conversation to which she might listen.

SAY IT JUST RIGHT CONVERSATION

Ivan catches Emily in the break room drinking a diet soda.

"Emily, I'm disappointed that you didn't get the designs back to us yesterday until nearly 4:00. This has happened three times, and it is really frustrating the team. We must get the designs back before noon on the day they are promised. I know you can do it because you've done it before." **(Specifies the problem behavior.)**

Emily looks up from the magazine she's flipping through. "I ran into a lot of traffic and just couldn't get back yesterday. What do you expect me to do?"

"I realize that you might have had some trouble getting back, but you left at 10. You did not return until 3:30. The fact is we must get the designs before noon. What can you do to get them here when we need them?" **(Invites Emily to talk without placing blame.)**

"I guess I could leave earlier."

"The production building is five blocks away. I do not see how leaving earlier will resolve the problem."

"Lois spends forever in the break room with her friends. I don't see why you are blaming me for not getting back sooner."

Ivan takes a deep breath. "I gave you this job because your father thought you could learn something. He had confidence in you, and I agreed to give you a chance. I'm beginning to think that I may have made the wrong decision. This might not be the best fit." **(Takes blame himself for making the wrong decision rather than placing blame on her.)**

Her eyes flash and she closes the magazine. "What are you saying?"

"I'm simply saying that we must get the designs before noon. If that is too difficult for you, then we need to find someone who can do that for us. We never had a problem with the interns we hired from the collage. Your father may need to find another spot for you in the firm. How do you feel about that?" **(States consequences.)**

"I like working here. It's just that I get so bored. All I do is copy lettering onto the designs and run errands. I am going crazy. My dad said I'd learn something about architecture. All I've learned is how to find the duplicating building."

"I hope you can understand my frustration, Emily. I'd love to give you more meaningful work to do. We've got hundreds of bushes and trees that need to be sketched into the two projects we got back yesterday. That might be something you could do. But, I can't give you any more tasks when you don't perform what I've already given you." **(Joins feelings with facts.)**

Her face brightens. "I'd love to draw some bushes and trees. I could do that. Please give me a chance."

Ivan shakes his head. "I can't give you a chance until I'm sure you will get the designs to us by noon. The reality is if we don't get them tomorrow, we will miss our deadline. I suspect your father will be very disappointed with all of us if that happens." **(Restates consequences.)**

She gets up. "I promise I will get the designs to you first thing tomorrow morning. Then, can I draw the bushes in those designs?"

"If you get those designs to us by no later than noon tomorrow, I will show you exactly how to insert the bushes and trees." (**Finds resolution with positive consequences.**)

Analysis

Will Emily remain committed to her job? Will she change her behavior? We do not know. But, Ivan did show compassion, and he did demonstrate curiosity. He also made the consequences clear. By not placing blame directly onto her, he managed to keep her from getting too defensive. When she finally stated her concerns about not learning anything about architecture, they worked out a solution. Ivan, however, reiterated what she must do in order to earn the chance to draw bushes and trees. His clarity on what he expected of her and what she must do to get more responsibility enabled him to *say it just right*.

Specify the Problem. Ivan repeated several times in the conversation that Emily must get the designs to the team by noon. He did not care how she did it or what caused such blatant lateness. He knew she often took shopping trips and visited with friends, but he did not mention these things. So long as the designs arrived in the office by noon, she would have done what he required. In a disciplinary conversation it is important not to get sidetracked and not to talk about too many infringements. Select the one thing you want corrected. If the other negative behaviors continue (and often they don't), you can deal with those in a later conversation.

Invite the Other Person to Talk. Emily responded defensively. She readily talked but in defense of her behavior. Even though Ivan did not say, "You are at fault," she knew she had abused her position on the job. Ivan invited Emily to tell her story in two places. The first occurred when he asked what happened yesterday and the second occurred after he stated the implied consequence that she might need to be transferred out of his department.

Join Feeling with Fact. Ivan, being a Technical, prefers not to share feelings. His EQ score is probably not terribly high. He knew, however, that he was dealing with an Expressive who responds well to feelings. In the first statement of the problem, Ivan said he was disappointed. He later stated his frustrations with her performance. He also mentioned Mr. Whippet's confidence in Emily and inferred that she might lose her father's respect if she could not get the designs back in time.

Resolve the Issue. Ivan listened to Emily when she talked about wanting to learn more about architecture. He played up this desire in his search for a resolution, which included positive consequences.

How to Tell Someone Something They Don't Want to Hear

In these times of layoffs and downsizing, many of us face the awkward position of having to tell someone they no longer have a job. This person may have been a valuable employee who performed satisfactorily or even extraordinarily. How can you tell someone who has done a good job that you no longer need his or her services?

Phil Harkins in *Powerful Conversations* provides us with some guidance on how to communicate bad information.[7] He suggests using the Powerful Conversation Model that he presented in his book. We can apply Harkins's model and expand on it with what we've learned about the SIJR Model to help guide us through these sticky situations:

Step 1: Ask questions to confirm understanding. This step requires honesty. Using the SIJR Model, you must say what you have to say in clear, direct language. Do not leave room for misunderstandings. If you are laying a person off, for example, do not let that person believe that you are temporarily suspending him. Do not let people believe there is something they can do to change your mind. Harkins also advises that when the information shocks the people, they cannot absorb it all at once.[8] You may need to give it some time before you proceed to the second step. Your own empathy and compassion in Step 1 will guide you to help the person move to Step 2.

Step 2: Harkins advises allowing the person to recognize that the facts, data, and statistics show that your company can no longer pay for his or her services or that the services are no longer necessary. Ask powerful, open questions that will reveal to you if the person understands the facts, data, and statistics. Harkins adds if you move to Step 3 before you are certain the person understands the facts and rationale behind the decision, he or she will not be open to new possibilities, and you'll find yourself making all the suggestions.

Step 3: Create new possibilities for action. Harkins suggests brainstorming with the person about new opportunities. Give the individual a chance to talk about what sounds possible for the future. As we've seen over and over with the SIJR Model, you need to encourage dialogue. Do not make all the suggestions and assume the person wants you to take control. Harkins adds that once all possibilities are clear, be willing to make calls or refer prospects.

Step 4: Join with the person to set up a clear action plan. How will you help with that plan? What will they do? What are the time frames? Finally, Harkins says one of the worst things you can do is leave someone feeling as if there is no place to turn. Make sure you clarify a plan and the person recognizes that this situation is not the end of the world. In the SIJR Model this facet occurs in the resolution stage where we work with the other person to resolve the issue in a manner that clarifies options.

Sticky Situation #11:
Telling Your Brother His Job is Gone

Robert teaches eleventh grade math. He's been teaching for nearly 15 years. Two years ago he purchased a bar/pool hall. This establishment was located in an excellent business district. Robert saw it as a chance to increase his income. When he first bought the property, he retained the previous managers of the bar, and they paid him rent on the building. Those managers, however, violated liquor licensing laws and vacated the premises. Once that happened, Robert faced two choices. He could either hire new managers or manage the bar himself. Since his school hours did not conflict with the bar hours, he chose the more profitable option: manage the bar himself.

Robert's older brother, Sam, is in his late fifties and looking for a lifestyle change. Because he and his wife love the community where Robert lives, Robert offered Sam the opportunity to move and to run the bar. Six months ago Sam started as the new bar manager.

Sam has done a great job running the daily operations of the bar. He hires and fires staff; he keeps the bar stocked with food and beverages; he manages the special evening events; he maintains the records. In fact, Sam does everything Robert has asked him to do. But, Robert has poured all his savings into the operation of the bar, and it still loses money every month. People come there to play pool and hang out but do not eat or drink enough to produce profits. Furthermore, Robert dumped quite a bit of money in the bar up front. He had to recarpet the building and to replace many of the pool tables and equipment. Financially, Robert is stretched beyond his limits, and his wife is pressuring him to sell the bar.

The bar is located on prime real estate. Robert could sell the bar and recoup all his out-of-pocket expenses. He won't come out on top of his investment, but at least he will recover his savings. With pressure from his wife, Robert finally agrees.

Robert must tell his brother that he will soon be out of work.

APPLYING THE SAY IT JUST RIGHT MODEL

DECISION POINTS

Robert weighs the costs. Robert knows that time has run out. He cannot continue to run the bar because he has no more money to put into it. Furthermore, the stress is killing him. He's losing sleep and working day and night. This venture is taking a toll on his health. He hates what he must say to Sam, but he has little choice. Sam came into the project knowing the risks. Robert told him that the bar had potential, but he could not predict if it would make it. Sam knew what he was getting into. Nonetheless, at Sam's age getting another job will prove difficult. He wants to work at least eight more years before he considers retirement. No matter how much Robert prepared Sam, this will be a blow.

Robert sets his limits. Robert knows that Sam will try and convince him to hold out a little longer. He recognizes that the bar will produce substantial profits someday, but perhaps not for Robert. Someone, who has the resources to pour into it and the income to wait, will likely reap the rewards. Robert has no choice, and he must help Sam see that. He plans to put the bar on the market at the end of the summer.

Robert examines power sources. On the surface Robert holds the power. He owns the bar and has the right to decide whether or not to sell it. He has the power to lay Sam off. On the other hand, Sam, as Robert's older brother, is someone he has always respected and admired. Because Robert respects Sam's opinions, Sam holds the power to dissuade him. Throughout his life, Robert has turned to Sam for advice and support. Ultimately, Robert faces the considerable challenge of not falling prey to Sam's efforts to convince him to stay in the business.

PERSONALITY OVERLAY

Robert is a Sympathetic personality. Even though he took the risk to purchase the bar, which was a bold move, that action was atypical for Robert. Being a Sympathetic, Robert thrives on making everyone happy. He wants to make his wife happy, and he wants to please his older brother. The purchase of the bar seemed like a good idea to him because it would ease the financial struggles in his family. Instead it worsened matters.

From what we know about Sam, it is hard for us to determine his personality style. We do know he took a huge risk when he moved to a strange town to begin a new job at his stage in life. That move took courage. Furthermore, from Robert's analysis, he seems to be a persuasive personality. The risky decisions to move here and to leave his long-time job suggest a Bold style. His persuasiveness suggests an Expressive style. A Technical would never leave a job in which he was eight years away from retiring and move to a new town. Finally, we see no behaviors that suggest Sam might or might not be a Sympathetic.

If Sam is a Bold it will be easier for Robert to talk to him. He can spell out the problem and go directly into the next steps. Sam will not want to hear a lot of detail. He will understand the need for action. Furthermore, the risky place Sam will find himself in will not pose as big a threat to a Bold as it might to the other personality styles.

If Sam is either an Expressive or a Sympathetic, it will be more difficult for Robert to talk to him. An Expressive will do everything in his power to convince Robert that he is making a mistake. He will use the power of his strong personality to change Robert's mind. A Sympathetic will exploit Robert's obligation as Sam's brother not to end his job and will tap into Robert's natural loyalty to his family. A Sympathetic could also become sad and depressed. Either of these styles or reactions will pose problems for Robert.

SAY IT JUST RIGHT CONVERSATION

On Sunday afternoon Robert walks into the bar where he's agreed to meet with his brother to talk.

"Sam, I want to discuss our finances. Things are not going well at the bar."

Sam jumps in. "I know. I know. I've got some ideas to turn all that around. I heard about a pool competition event that we can hook up with. Green Brier Billiards used to sponsor it every year, but they're not going to do it anymore. I think they're nearly bankrupt. Anyway, this is a great chance for us to get a huge boost."

"Sam, I'm finished. I don't think you get it. I can't go on. I brought the figures in for you to look at for yourself. This will show you how much debt I've gotten myself into. I simply can't put any more money in it. It's gotten way out of control. I've decided I have no choice but to sell the bar." **(Specifies the problem with facts and statistics.)**

"Come on, Robbie, you can hang in there longer. Everybody knows it takes more than two years to get a new business going. Look at the statistics. Remember when dad started the car shop? He nearly went bankrupt in the first few years. But, then everything evened out. Most small businesses don't make any money in the first two years. We've actually made a little, particularly since I've been here. You've only had control of the bar for eight months. Give it a couple of years and you'll have more money than you can count. This place has real potential. You know it and so do I."

Robert gets up and paces around the room. "I don't have two years. I can't borrow any more money without going bankrupt. It's over for me. I'm going to put the bar on the market at the end of August."

"I can't believe you're quitting. You're not a quitter. I've never known you to just give up like this. What you need is a good accountant who can help you shift money around. I've got a guy I worked with in Philly. Let me give him a call. He knows how to work miracles. I bet he's just what you need. There's no need to rush into this decision."

"Sam, you are not listening to what I am saying. What have I just said to you?" **(Asks questions to confirm understanding—Step 1.)**

"You said you are quitting. That's what I've heard."

"No, Sam, that's not what I said. I said I have no more resources. The money is gone. I'd love to keep going, and if I had the resources, I would. But, I don't, and you don't either. We've got to face reality. We can't keep this place operating. I'm very sad that you got mixed up in this with me. I would give anything if you had not come down here, but you are here. We must figure out what you are going to do." **(Joins feelings with facts.)**

"Remember when you were a kid and you didn't want to go to camp that first year, and dad made you go? I'll never forget walking you up the dirt path. I had to nearly push you. But once you got there, you loved it. Remember? This is the same thing. I'll be here to help you out, Robbie. We can get through this. The two of us could conquer the world."

Robert sighs. "This isn't camp. I know you want to believe that I can get through this, but I've looked at every option. I brought the books for you to examine for yourself. Sam, you can't talk me out of this, the bar is going on the market in August. I've already listed it with a Realtor. I have no choice." (**Confirms action with statistics, facts—Step 2.**)

Sam wipes the sweat from his forehead. He gets up and walks toward the window and studies the books. "I just know I could've made this place go."

"Yeah, I know you could've, too. It's just I can't be there to support it. I'm sorry I let you down, Sam."

They both remain quiet for several minutes.

"Let's talk about what you might do," Robert says. (**Invites Sam to look at possibilities—Step 3.**)

"What's there to talk about? I'm going to stay here. Maybe the new owners will want me to continue. I don't see I have a choice."

"That's certainly a possibility but probably a temporary one. You can't be sure the new owners won't want to bring in their own management. Let's look at some other alternatives. What else might you like to do?"

"Look, Robbie, at my age I just can't start polishing up my résumé. Nobody wants to hire an old guy like me. Furthermore, who do I know in this town? You and all your friends? That's about it. If I don't stay at the bar, I'm lost."

"It seems that way now. But look, Sam, you've already made many connections here. You've got so much talent. If you hadn't moved, what had you intended to do? You weren't happy in your old job. Surely there was something else you considered doing."

"Well, I explored starting a Web design business, but I never really gave it serious thought."

"Maybe that's an option for you. The school is looking for someone to handle technology, but they don't want to hire a full-time person. Maybe you'd like to give that a go considering all the technology experience you've got."

Sam's shoulders rise slightly. "I suppose I could look at developing a contract business and work out of our house."

"You could do that even if you stay at the bar for a while. Let's make a plan of action." (**Resolving the issue and co-creating an action plan—Step 4.**)

Sam pulls out a blank piece of paper. "If you sell the bar this year, I'd better have something by early October. That gives me five months. That's doable. I'll put together a business plan and a list of potential contacts." He makes notes on the sheet. "Actually, a Web business does not have to have a local focus. I could include my contacts in Philly. I actually investigated doing this before I came here."

"Lots of people hated to see you move away. I bet you can secure at least two contracts by October. Meantime, I'll get you in touch with my principal. I know he'll want to talk to you. Also, Sam, when the bar is sold, I can pay you back the money you put into it. That will make a nice nest egg for you until you get your business started."

Sam gets up. "Are you sure about all this? You can still change your mind."

Robert grins. "No, I'm not changing my mind, big brother."

"Well, if that's how it must be, I'll survive, and so will you. We'll get through this just like we've done everything else in our lives."

They embrace.

ANALYSIS

Robert did what he had to do and did not falter. He dealt with Sam's unwillingness to face the facts by showing compassion, by asking powerful questions, and by sticking to his decision. Once Sam realized that belittling Robert by calling him a quitter or falling back on their family history would not work, he gave in. Robert followed the SIJR Model incorporating the four steps Harkins suggested in giving bad news and managed to *say it just right.*

Specify the Problem. Early in the conversation, Robert told Sam he was going to sell the business and he told him why. He had facts to justify his decision. Robert did not say, "I'm thinking about selling the business," or "I'm considering what to do about my debt." Instead, he said, "I'm going to sell the bar." His decision was clear and not up for negotiation.

Invite the Other Person to Talk. Because Sam is clearly an Expressive, inviting him to talk was not difficult. In the beginning Sam jumped in with ideas about why Robert was making the wrong decision. He quickly showed Robert he should change his mind, and he'd be there to support him. Later, when he realized Robert would not change his mind and his options were running out, Sam grew quieter. Robert asked powerful questions and showed a lot of compassion to get Sam to look at future possibilities.

Join Feelings with Facts. Robert revealed his feelings of exhaustion and sadness. He linked those feelings with the facts throughout the conversation. When Sam tried to force him to keep going, Robert came back with feelings. These feelings strengthened his decision to sell the bar. In one instance Robert said he wished he could keep the place going, and he regretted bringing Sam into the business. Both these statements of feeling demonstrated to Sam Robert's extreme sense of loss. Being a Sympathetic, it was easy for Robert to talk about his feelings in a genuine manner.

Resolve the Issue. Once Sam clearly heard Robert and was ready to look at options, they both discussed the future. In accordance with Harkins's model, Robert offered to help Sam launch a new business. Reminding Sam of the money that will come back to him when the bar is sold helped Sam see this was not the end of the world. When Sam began to think about possibilities himself, Robert knew Sam heard him and was ready to move forward.

CONCLUSION

In this chapter we looked at sticky situations with subordinates. We examined those situations in light of disciplinary conversations and conversations where leaders must deliver bad information. We selected two particularly difficult examples: the first with the boss's daughter and the second with a close relative. Whether or not you are dealing with relatives of your superiors or with people with whom you are close, if you carefully go through the processes we've shared, you can *say it just right*. As you manage and lead more people in your career, you will take more risks and find yourself face-to-face with many kinds of situations—employees who lie, employees who steal, having to fire people, and giving negative information to your boss, to name a few. You can conduct successful conversations if you approach each of these situations using the SIJR Model. Nonetheless, your skill as a leader will be tested each time.

In Chapters 3 through 6 of the book, we dealt with sticky situations involving a sector of people, bosses, co-workers, customers, and subordinates. The remaining chapters explore sticky situations that are situational in nature. Chapter 7 looks at sticky situations in meetings or in team settings where we must apply the SIJR Model in light of group dynamics.

NOTES

1. See www.gallup.com.

2. Brad Gilbreath and Philip Benson, "The Contribution of Supervisor Behavior to Employee Psychological Well-Being," *Work & Stress* 18, no. 3 (2004): 255–66.

3. Daniel Goleman, Richard Boyatzis, and Annie McKee, *Primal Leadership: Learning to Lead with Emotional Intelligence* (Boston: Harvard Business School Press, 2002).

4. The Arbinger Institute, *Leadership and Self-Deception: Getting Out of the Box* (San Francisco: Berrett-Koehler Publishers, 2000).

5. Douglas Stone, Bruce Patton, and Sheila Heen, *Difficult Conversations: How to Discuss What Matters Most* (New York: Penguin Books, 1999).

6. Ibid., 61.

7. Phil Harkins, *Powerful Conversations: How High Impact Leaders Communicate* (New York: McGraw Hill, 1999), 75.

8. Ibid., 77.

Chapter 7

Sticky Situations in Meetings

One person severely criticizes another during a staff meeting. People clam up and do not contribute during a team meeting. Cliques sabotage the efforts of the team. These kinds of sticky situations plague many leaders. Becoming a competent team facilitator is a necessary skill in today's business world. Managing effectively one on one isn't enough anymore; you must also manage groups both face to face and virtually. Before we examine the way the SIJR Model works in group settings, let's look at the common components in all groups as well as what defines a group.

What Is a Group?

Two or more people define a group. This definition tells us that it takes at least two people to make a team, not necessarily a high-performing team, but a team. Couples, therefore, are teams. What number produces a high functioning team? Studies tell us that seven people form an ideal team size. Why?

- Too few people do not have enough data among them to produce high-functioning results. One main purpose of a team is to bring in new and different ideas. As the old Japanese proverb says, "None of us is as smart as all of us."

- Too many people create chaos. When teams reach 10 to 20 members, they no longer form teams, but large groups or crowds (depending on size). Such large numbers limit team participation. Many people do not fully engage because in large groups how can everyone share?

Components of High-Performance Teams

High-performance teams require more than just a magic number. To function at peak levels, teams must also have common goals, shared norms, and interlocking needs.

- **Common Goals** implies that team members do not have the *same* goal, but they share goals in common. One of the first jobs of any team is to reconcile the differences between and among the individual goals and the team goal in order to reach common ground.

- **Shared Norms.** What is a norm? Simply put, a norm reflects an unspoken behavior. People do not talk about norms because they are supposed to know the norms without talking about them. For example, when people enter a room for the first time, where do they sit? Norms tell us to sit in a vacant chair. In certain cultures, however, we might sit on a large pillow. Norms are the things we do without thinking. We expect others to do the same things. When others do something else, we shut them out. Another example of how norms work: Some women do not understand male kidding around. They take offense when a man teases them. When the woman shows her offense, the man shrugs it off and thinks *this person isn't one of us.* In today's global economy, norms have taken a new and a more prominent role. It is important for us to not only recognize when our norms differ but also to search for ways to work together rather than shut each other out. One of my clients works for a large technology company that employs programmers in India. She discovered that the Indian programmers never say they cannot meet a deadline. No matter how absurd the deadline, they always say they can meet it. Knowing she could not directly ask them if they could meet a deadline because they'd always say, "yes," she posed questions such as, "What will you have to do to meet this deadline?" or, "What resources are necessary to meet this deadline?" She had to adjust her norms to fit the norms of the Indian programmers.

- **Interlocking Needs.** Team members need one another. I need you and you need me. I can't win without you. If I feel I can win without you, I will not do what I must do to be part of the team. If I feel I can do a better job on a project alone, I will not push myself to be part of a team.

In the early stages of team formation members struggle with goals, norms, and conflicting needs. Until they resolve those issues, "teams" do not exist. What exists instead is simply a group of individuals. Often sticky situations in meetings occur during this struggle.

In addition to common goals, shared norms, and interlocking needs, groups go through certain clear stages of development. Understanding these stages helps us recognize what to do when and how to keep from igniting sticky situations. Similarly to a child who is maturing, teams call for nurturing in order to grow strong in the early stages of development.

THE TEAM DEVELOPMENT PROCESS

In the mid-1960s, Bruce Tuckman studied the way teams work and noticed emerging patterns. These patterns became the crux of today's team theory. Tuckman demonstrated that all teams go through certain stages of growth and that within those stages there exist certain things that team members can do and certain things that they are not yet ready to do.[1] Think of your team as a new baby. You wouldn't ask your new baby to tell you when he feels hungry or to let you know when he has to go to the bathroom. Most sticky situations within groups occur because we ask a team to do something it is not ready to do. Knowledge of the stages of team development can minimize frustration and maximize growth and high achievement.

TUCKMAN'S STAGES OF TEAM DEVELOPMENT

- **Forming.** In first stage of team development a group of individuals come together with little knowledge of each other. In this stage members want to be part of the team, but they also pull away. Their desire to be part of the team typifies our human desire for belonging. At the same time, individuals fear they will lose their persona. Some people call this stage approach/avoidance. Members wonder if the other team members will accept them and their ideas. Members question the motives of others. Psychologically they do not wish to be absorbed by this team. The task a team at the forming stage can perform adequately is *Orientation* to each other and to the mission of the team.

- **Storming.** The second stage of team development is often identified as the most uncomfortable for any team. Although members now recognize the value of the team itself, they also want others to notice and respect their own *individual* value. Imagine everyone on the team vying for attention. Members unseat each other for power and control. Instead of listening to other members, people talk about their own experiences and knowledge. The initial fear of being overlooked that surfaced in the Forming Stage becomes the guiding motive for the Storming Stage. The only task teams can adequately perform at this stage is *Organization* of the conflicting struggles around the team goals. For example imagine a team that wants to create a group slogan. That team might organize around each individual's strengths. Who has developed slogans in the past? Who is good at limericks? Who considers themselves creative? What other skills are needed to help us develop the slogan? Rather than look at what the slogan needs to say, the team organizes itself around individual strengths. Such organization enables team members to share information about themselves. As they share and as they listen, members learn who is best suited to do what.

- **Norming.** The third stage of team development feels very comfortable to team members, but it can also be one of the most dangerous stages in the process. In the Norming Stage team members no longer disagree. They support each other in everything. Members acknowledge one another with statements like, "That's a great idea," or, "I really like what you are saying." Maintaining group intimacy becomes the motivation of the team. The biggest danger this team faces is a phenomenon called *groupthink*. The term groupthink came out of sociological research before and during the Bay of Pigs incident in 1961.[2]

  Shortly after John F. Kennedy became president, he faced the decision of whether or not to invade Cuba. The previous administration had been about to launch a preemptive strike on the island. Kennedy wondered if such action was in the best interest of the United States. He called together key national advisors and asked each one what he thought. All the advisors wanted to do what everyone else wanted to do. They did not wish to "rock the boat." Instead of sharing their concerns about the outcome of such an invasion, they agreed to the operation known as the Bay of Pigs. Today, in hindsight, we know that operation failed. Simply defined, groupthink is when everyone decides to do something stupid together. In the Norming Stage groups are not yet ready to make decisions. Instead they are quite adept at *Data Flow*, or open sharing without evaluation. In this stage groups generate creative ideas.

- **Performing.** The fourth stage happens when the group members recognize each other's strengths and weaknesses. Each person willingly listens to one another with renewed respect. The ability to share strengths and weaknesses leads the group to its most important task, that is, *Problem Solving*. Members finally reach the highly performing stage where they can address problems in a different way—through the eyes of the team—rather than through the eyes of individuals. Problem solving becomes fun. A new synergy forms that enables the team to tackle more challenges and reach high levels of performance.

- **Adjourning.** The final stage of team development occurs after team members finish their task and are ready to evaluate their work and close up shop. The team begins the task of *Evaluation* on two fronts: First, they consider the team's success. How did we do as a team? How did others respond to our work? Would we want to work together again? Second, they evaluate their individual success. Did the group accept me? Did I feel comfortable in the group? How was my input received?

Understanding the stages of group development and the tasks associated with each stage help prevent many group-related sticky situations. Unfortunately, the process is not orderly. Unlike a child who goes from babyhood to toddler to teen, groups sometimes skip steps or get stuck in one stage and can't find their way out. All groups begin at the Forming Stage and logically they end at the Adjourning Stage. With those exceptions, the process is unpredictable and depends on the individuals who come together. For example, some groups never come out of the Forming Stage. They stay in that awkward, unsure place the entire time the group meets. Other groups get stuck in the Storming Stage. They argue every point. They lose site of the overall mission of the team and must be reminded of it over and over. They do not complete tasks because they have no commitment to do so. Still other teams go from Forming to Norming and then to Storming. This forward-backward path frustrates team members because they enjoyed the Norming Stage. They often lash out at the circumstance or person who pushed them into the Storming Stage. Battles in the Storming Stage often result in the loss of group members.

The next few pages examine sticky situations in meetings. We will determine what stage of team development the group is in and how that stage affects the team members before we apply the SIJR Model.

How Good a Team Player Are You?

Answer True or False to the following 10 statements.

1. I come to meetings 5 to 10 minutes late.
2. I am the first one at each meeting.
3. When team members disagree, I find myself siding with the same people.
4. I truly believe I could be more successful without the bother of team work.
5. I am often selected to lead the team or to take a prominent role on the team.
6. When everyone on the team agrees, I tend to agree, too.
7. When the team reaches a decision but I have doubts, I voice my concerns.
8. I look at my watch often during team meetings.
9. When things are not clear, I ask questions.
10. If I think someone on the team is left out, I try to include them.

Get your results in Appendix 1.

Sticky Situation #12:
A Major Client Storms Out of the Room

Reuben owns a medium-sized interior decoration firm, which specializes in corporate buildings and medium-sized hotels. Reuben likes to work with a team of professionals, including the architect, the contractor, and his own design staff. Last week Reuben sold a proposal to a new client. The client, FJ Lewis, represents a large mortgage firm, headquartered in London but beginning to relocate to the United States. FJ hired Reuben along with the architect and contractor, independently. None of the parties have worked together on previous projects. Reuben asked FJ to call a meeting so they could begin the job in a team atmosphere.

The meeting convened in Reuben's conference room. The architect, Marsha Malone, arrived first. Reuben gave her a short tour of his offices while they waited for the other members. During that time, she asked Reuben a number of questions about his design experience. Soon after, the contractor arrived, accompanied by his top foreman. They settled in the conference room, drinking coffee and chatting while they waited for FJ. After about 10 minutes Marsha rolled out a blueprint. "I've talked extensively to FJ and drew up these preliminary plans to get us started."

"You can't take out a column there," the contractor said, pointing to the main entrance. "That will cause structural problems. I know that building. I worked on it when it was erected 15 years ago. Not only that, but the city will never let you go that high."

The architect responded by defending her plans and specifying the structural components that fit with FJ's requirements. Meanwhile Reuben jumped in the fray. "FJ wants something more modern than this," he said and began talking about what kinds of projects his company designed in the past that captured a more modern feel.

Five minutes later FJ bustled in and tossed his brief case on the table.

The architect spoke first. "There's some controversy among us over the plans you and I discussed. I put something together based on the numbers and measurements we talked about."

"You simply can't take out a column there, and the city will never let you build this kind of structure in the downtown corridor," the contractor butted in.

Reuben interrupted him and remarked that his firm prided itself on modern décor and this structure looked more American colonial. He didn't think that was what FJ was asking for. The contractor rose and began pacing the room. While he described the large-scale projects his firm has worked on and what he knows about the building FJ purchased for this project, Marsha interrupted with pointed questions. Reuben could tell that FJ was getting increasingly agitated.

"That's it," FJ cut in. "If you guys want to argue, go duke it out someplace else. I don't have time for this." He gathered his stuff and stormed out the door.

Stages of Team Development

The team Reuben wants to put together is brand new. The members do not know one another nor are they clear on the purpose of the meeting. Undoubtedly this team began in the Forming Stage.

Looking at interlocking needs, we see that no one on this team can complete this large-scale project alone. The architect needs the contractor and the design team to do her job. The contractor must work closely with the architect to do his job. The design team must coordinate with both the architect and the contractor. Furthermore, everyone must reach some agreement about what the client needs. Group members tried to impress one another with their particular credentials and by so doing quickly moved out of the Forming Stage and into the Storming Stage. Meanwhile, they lost the client.

What caused the group to move so quickly out of the Forming Stage? As soon as the architect pulled out the preliminary plans, the group reacted with negative feedback. Not having a chance to orient themselves to one another nor to the project, members went immediately into the Storming Stage. It became a group in panic mode.

This analysis of the group and what it needs to do enables Reuben to apply the SIJR Model and reconstruct the meeting.

Applying the Say It Just Right Model

Decision Points

Reuben weighs the costs. Reuben recognizes that his effort to create a team atmosphere failed. He is not sure he likes either the architect or the contractor and would prefer to work with people he knows. If, however, he tries to convince FJ to use other firms, he may lose FJ altogether. Apparently Marsha Malone and FJ have worked together in the past. Reuben has a successful business, but he recognizes the need to keep new clients coming in. This project would boost Reuben's business to another level.

Reuben sets limits. Reuben cannot work with an architect and a contractor who do not get along. He's experienced that nightmare in the past and vowed never to do that again. When he heard that both the architect and the builder did not know one another, Reuben predicted trouble. Working under these conditions is not an option. The architect and the contractor must connect before Reuben can do his job. He decides to talk to FJ to determine if he still wants to contract with Reuben's company. If he does, then Reuben will agree to meet once more with the architect and the contractor. If that meeting also fails, Reuben cannot agree to participate on the project.

Reuben examines the power sources. Reuben believes FJ has all the power. He has put a huge project to the table. If this project succeeds, Reuben could double his revenues. On the other hand, Reuben offers a unique talent. The design community regards Reuben's firm highly for its state-of-the-art creativity in modern structures. Reuben knows that FJ admires his reputation and will be hard pressed to find a firm of equal quality and reliability.

PERSONALITY OVERLAY

Understanding the different personalities in any group is very important. Imagine a group of all Bolds, for example. During the Forming Stage, Reuben must examine the individual behaviors in order to ascertain the personality styles represented. Marsha Malone brought plans to the meeting, and she responded to questions with facts and structural elements. She is likely a Technical. The contractor interrupted the architect while speaking and at one point he got up and paced the room. Those behaviors suggest a Bold personality. FJ might be an Expressive personality because he seemed uncomfortable and impatient with the arguing. Had he been a Bold, he would have simply told the others to be quiet and stated his position.

SIJR CONVERSATION LEADING TO A SECOND MEETING

Reuben places a call to FJ an hour after the meeting abruptly ended.

"I apologize that the group meeting failed this morning. How do you propose we proceed?" he asks. **(Invites FJ to talk.)**

FJ says, "Are you willing to work with my people?"

"My problem is I need cooperation between the major players, in this case the architect and the contractor. I did not see that this morning, but I don't believe we gave it a chance. It seemed to me when you met with the architect before we all had a chance to talk, you unwittingly shut out both my input and that of the contractor. For us to work as a team, we all need to be on the same page. What is your take on this?" **(Specifies the problem and sets limits.)**

"My boss calls me every day. He wants to see some measurable progress. It took me months to identify the best players for this job. I'm confident I found them in each of these firms. Marsha and I briefly discussed what I'd like to see. I had no idea she'd come armed with preliminary plans. I'm sure, however, she was responding to pressure from me to get this thing off the ground."

"It takes time for people to develop a trusting working relationship. I'm as frustrated as you are. I was excited and enthusiastic to be a part of this project. It's a great opportunity for my firm. I have to say, however, I cannot be part of any team that doesn't cooperate. I've learned that lesson the hard way. I don't have time to do things over and over because the architect and the contractor or the contractor and the client disagree. That was why I wanted us to meet in the first place." (**Joins feelings with facts and respecifies the problem with consequences.**)

"I sure as hell don't want to waste time or money doing anything over. Let's try and meet again. I'll contact Marsha and tell her not to draw up any plans until we all have a chance to talk. How does that sound?" (**Client suggests a resolution.**)

They agree to meet the next day at the same time.

Analysis

Let's examine how Reuben handled the conversation with FJ. By apologizing in the beginning, he softened FJ, who may have still been angry over the failed morning meeting.

Specify the Problem. Instead of specifying the problem immediately, Reuben began by inviting FJ to share how he'd like to proceed. Reuben took a risk in doing this. FJ might have said that he wanted to fire all three firms and find someone else. Reuben trusted his reputation and determined that FJ wanted to hear another option. Once FJ asked the question, "Are you willing to work with my people?" it was clear to Reuben that FJ not only wanted to keep him but was also willing to discuss options. At that point Reuben specified the problem and set his limits.

Invite the Other Person to Talk. Reuben invited FJ to talk immediately when he asked him how he wanted to proceed. He listened while FJ discussed the pressure his boss was putting on him.

Join Feeling with Fact. Reuben shared his frustration with FJ as well as his enthusiasm to work on this project. He stated that he couldn't work with players who fought among themselves. He combined the consequences with his feelings.

Resolve the Issue. FJ came up with the resolution. Reuben listened to FJ and shared his position enabling FJ to agree to a second meeting. When a client storms out of a meeting, the clear goal is to get the client to meet again.

SAY IT JUST RIGHT MEETING

The architect and the contractor rode up in the elevator together to Reuben's office. FJ came in five minutes later. Reuben convened the meeting.

"I realize our last meeting got off on the wrong foot. I've talked to each of you separately, and everyone agreed we should start over. This time, let's begin by hearing from FJ. We are all anxious to understand his vision for the project before we begin."

FJ spends the next 10 minutes talking about what he wants to accomplish with the building renovation. Both the architect and contractor ask questions. When FJ finishes, Reuben says, "Because none of us have worked together in the past, let's spend a few minutes talking about how we like to work and what value we bring to the project."

Following this discussion, the group members talk about the next steps. They each describe what they need in order to begin working and they plan a follow-up meeting at the site.

ANALYSIS

Reuben does not expect the group members to agree on everything. Each comes to the project with differing needs and artistic orientations. His second attempt at the meeting, however, enabled the group to orient itself around the client's mission. During that second meeting they also discovered each other's strengths and abilities. Having already "stormed" they may very well move into the Norming Stage without further storming. Once they begin disagreeing with respect, in other words, listening to each other's suggestions and searching for creative solutions, they will have moved into the Performing Stage.

STICKY SITUATION #13:
CLIQUES THAT SABOTAGE

Eight months ago, Karl began as the executive director for a small nonprofit whose mission is to provide camping experiences for underprivileged children. Camp Free For All began six years earlier when a generous woman in the community opened her private home to children during the months of June and July. During the early years the camp grew and began winning a number of grants. The camp now partners with a local park for use of its facilities. Four years ago a board formed with people who have been involved with the camp from its inception. This year, three of the nine board members rotated off and three new members joined the group. During board meetings Karl notices that the six longer-serving members form a very tight clique. They never vote against each other. The current board chairman, Karen, is a very good friend of Camp Free For All's founder, and she has donated much of her own money to the camp. Another long-serving board member, Brenda, has worked hard to raise money for the camp. Her husband, Daniel, serves as the treasurer of the board and handles all the computer operations for the camp. Each board member actively contributes either time or money to the operations of the camp. Karl concedes that this organization began informally, but he also knows he must take charge of the operational functions in order for the camp to grow as he envisions and as the board embraced when they hired him.

During the board meeting, Karl presents the budget in which he requests a part-time development position and a part-time administrative assistant. If he manages to fill these two positions, he will gain control of fund-raising as well as administrative operations. While making an impassioned plea to the board in favor of these positions, he notices three board members whispering to one another and shaking their heads. Three more stare at him with glazed eyes as if they were uninterested. The three newest members smile and nod at him with both interest and approval.

"Well," says Jack, one of the new board members, "this is a no-brainer. Karl has done a good job in presenting what he needs. We should do our job and give it to him. Let's go ahead and vote."

Karen grins at Brenda and says, "Let's see if there is any discussion?"

"In my opinion the camp has done quite well without hiring a bunch of people. Our numbers increase every year. Brenda does a good job with writing grants. We got two new ones awarded to us this year. I always say don't fix it if it ain't broke. I would not support hiring people at this juncture," Daniel says.

"I agree," Karen says with a nod. "We know that you have big plans for the camp, Karl, and we don't want to stand in your

way, but we've got to exercise a little restraint. You really have no idea how much each of us has put into this camp. I used to bring homemade cookies to the kids every afternoon, and Sandi Smith and Brenda made cherry pies and took the kids out for ice cream. This isn't your typical camp. It's more like a family."

Two more board members speak up in support of Karen.

Karl protests, saying two part-time positions are not exorbitant requests given that he hopes to double the camp's revenues and thereby increase its capacity and outreach.

Brenda calls for the vote. The new budget with the two new positions loses six to three. Karl leaves the meeting, crushed.

STAGE OF TEAM DEVELOPMENT

The board that existed before the new members entered was probably a group that had advanced to the Performing Stage. Once groups get to Performing, they strive to stay there. When the three new board members and the new executive director joined the group, the group returned to the Forming Stage. The longtime members now function at the Norming Stage and the new members at the Forming Stage. These two stages struggle against each other. When this happens it is common for cliques to form. Cliques are smaller groups within the group often at a higher level of team development than the group as a whole. Unfortunately cliques typify Storming groups.

Karl's proposal for two new positions reached beyond what a team at the Storming Stage can adequately address. Storming is a time for organization, not decision making. Now that Karl understands group dynamics, he is in a position to more successfully introduce his new endeavors.

APPLYING THE SAY IT JUST RIGHT MODEL

DECISION POINTS

Karl weighs the costs. Karl accepted this position because he loved the idea of helping children experience the pleasure of camp. From his first day of work, he bubbled with enthusiasm about what he could accomplish. He realizes now that the proposal he put before the board was too aggressive. His own impatience to serve as many children as possible clouded his judgment. Unfortunately for Karl, he is not the only one who is frustrated. The three new board members, particularly

Jack, are losing patience with the rest of the board. The last vote clearly illustrated the board divisions. If Karl does nothing and allows things to go on as they always have, he will probably lose his job and the new board members. He does not wish to work for people who micromanage. The responsibility of this board is policy making, not hands-on daily activities. If Karl acts, he might also lose his job, but he will have made it easier for his successor.

Karl sets the limits. Karl recognizes his mistake in presenting the board with two new positions when he's been on the job for less than a year. He decides to give in on one of those positions, the development job. He must, however, wrestle the administrative functions from Daniel. It makes no sense to Karl for Daniel, a volunteer, to have as much hands-on responsibility. The camp has grown beyond that stage. Karl will agree to give up the request for the development position but not for the administrative assistant.

Karl determines the power sources. The board has the ultimate power. The board hired Karl, and they can fire him. The board decides whether or not to fund the budget. Where does that leave Karl? If you ask Karl, he'd tell you he has no power and that the ultimate authority lies with the board. Karl knows, however, that the board went through an extensive and exhausting search before hiring him. It took them months to find the right person. He suspects that they will not want to go through that process again. Furthermore, the board likes his innovative ideas. They share his enthusiasm for expanding the camp.

PERSONALITY OVERLAY

Karl's Bold personality pushed him to launch his ideas prematurely. Presenting such an aggressive budget to a board that was clearly not yet cohesive was a big risk. Bolds often take big risks, sure that they will succeed. The other group members represent a mixture of the styles. Brenda seems to be a Sympathetic. She is loyal to the camp and willing to go along with anything the other board members want. Daniel appears more Technical. He looks at logical reasons to make decisions and prefers not to make changes (don't fix what's not broken). Karen seems more Expressive. She likes being center stage and prefers the persuasive role behind the scenes. Jack, the new board member, demonstrates Bold characteristics because he wanted to cast his vote without discussion. Jack will clearly have trouble serving on this board if he is routinely left out of the informal decision-making channels.

SAY IT JUST RIGHT MEETING

Karen calls a special meeting of the board at Karl's request.

"I appreciate your taking time from your busy schedules for this meeting," Karl begins. "Our last meeting left me feeling frustrated. Because I'm so excited about what we can accomplish at Camp Free For All, I wanted to get together again and see if we can iron out our differences." **(Joins feeling with fact and specifies the problem.)**

"We aren't differing with you, Karl," says Brenda. "It's just that we want to take things a bit slower."

"I get that. I put too much in front of you at once. You weren't ready for such an aggressive move. I misunderstood, thinking that's why you hired me, but apparently I was moving too fast. I'm curious to know what your vision for the camp is. I've shared mine, but it occurred to me that this board has never set a vision." **(Invites the board to talk.)**

Members start talking about what they want for the camp. Long-time members reminisce about the early days. While they talk, Karl tosses in questions for clarification. Everyone participates and soon the energy level in the room rises. People laugh. They joke with one another. Karl feels the shift. At the end, they come up with a joint vision statement that everyone endorses. Jack recommends that they put that statement on all their printed materials, and everyone agrees.

Karl asks about meeting informally for a few weeks until they all get more comfortable with each other. "I want to maintain the energy I feel in the room today." **(Resolves the problem.)**

ANALYSIS

Karl does not expect the clique to disappear overnight. He hopes, however, to dilute it by bringing the other board members into the discussion. If the clique continues to dominate, he may have to address that problem separately by talking to Karen and soliciting her support to put a stop to the informal discussions outside the scheduled meetings.

Karl did several good things when he reconvened. He took responsibility for the failed board meeting. He attributed the problems to his own newness to the board. Then, he opened up discussion, and he listened quietly while members spoke. He also gave the old board members an opportunity to share the history of the camp. Doing so helped the newer members, himself included, to gain an understanding of the camp's culture. He did not bring up his desire to hire the administrative assistant. He now recognizes that he cannot broach decision making until this board is ready. The heightened energy and sharing will move the group into the Norming Stage. If Karl exercises patience (which is hard for a Bold), he will gain the trust of the board and be able to assume the administrative operations of the camp.

STICKY SITUATION #14:
THE VIRTUALLY IMPOSSIBLE TEAM

Albert works for an international wireless company. He's been recently given the job of managing a virtual team of 53 IT professionals. Their project is to roll out a new software application to 45,000 employees throughout the world. Albert recognizes that his team consists of busy professionals doing other things. His project adds one more task to their already overflowing plate. Furthermore, his boss told him that the timeline is uncompromising. They must have the software rolled out in eight weeks, and they cannot request additional resources to do so.

Albert divided the larger project team into five geographical work groups. These virtual groups represent different parts of the company in different parts of the world. After Albert assigned certain managers and technicians to each group, he scheduled the first virtual group meeting by telephone. During that meeting he explained the project. He listened to their complaints about the short time frame and how the project will disrupt business, but he did not respond to these concerns. He has now set up another conference call to begin planning the rollout in phases even though he knows the groups are still contentious.

STAGE OF TEAM DEVELOPMENT

Albert is working with five virtual teams in the Forming Stage. In the first meeting he oriented each smaller group to the project itself. He allowed them to vent, but he did not give them ample time to orient to each other within their smaller groups. As Albert sees it, he must focus on his agenda; otherwise, they will overshoot the timeline. Albert's job is on the line. He agreed to take responsibility for this project, and he must show leadership to enable the teams to accomplish the overall goal. If he pushes the teams into decision making too soon, he will create more anger and bickering. To move the groups successfully through the team development process, he will have to go from orientation to organization.

Applying the Say It Just Right Model

Decision Points

Albert sets limits. Albert's boss told him the timeline is uncompromising. Albert realizes that to make the eight-week deadline, he must include people who have successfully worked together before. He cannot waste too much time on group wrangling. He decides to stipulate to his boss that he must select 75 percent of the teams. Albert knows there are certain people in the company who will work with him to make this project succeed. If his boss does not allow him to tap those people, Albert will tell his boss he cannot manage this project. Fortunately for Albert, his boss agreed to this stipulation.

Albert weighs the costs. Albert knows that he must get the project completed in eight weeks. He assembled teams of people with whom he has worked in the past. He trusts them to do whatever it takes to get through the project. He also included people in the organization who are necessary to make the rollout run smoothly. If the rollout succeeds, Albert will reap the rewards and gain respect as a team leader. If the teams fail, Albert, too, will fail. The costs are high.

Albert examines the power sources. Albert knows that this project is one more thing added to his "to-do" list. His boss is stretching him beyond what both of them realize is possible. Albert's boss needs him to take on this project. There is no one else in the company with as much success with project teams as Albert. He and his boss know that. Albert feels as if he has earned his boss's respect as a project team manager. Albert knows that the teams have the ultimate power. If the teams succeed, so will Albert. Recognizing the teams' power puts Albert in a position to respond to the teams' needs rather than push his own agenda.

Personality Overlay

Because Albert works for a large wireless company in the IT area, it is probable that he has several Technicals on his teams. Albert, himself, might be a Technical. As such, he wants to get the job done as effectively as possible while the other Technicals may strive for perfection. Technicals are never satisfied because they search for that magic formula that spells perfection. It is up to Albert to push them out of stagnation. The makeup of Albert's teams will make this task either harder or easier. Those people who have high backup styles in either Bold or Expressive will help move the project forward. Being virtual teams, Albert will not have the ability to read verbal cues. He will have to depend on vocal messages. This makes reading the group dynamics even more challenging.

CONDUCTING A VIRTUAL MEETING USING THE SIJR MODEL

Albert begins his meeting with his team responsible for the European rollout by stating his desire to stick to the agenda. One of the top regional managers in the group interrupts, "We need to pick up where we left off last time. We can't even think about how to initiate the rollout until we determine what we are going to roll out. It's been my experience that rolling out the entire system at once is suicidal. We need to introduce pieces and go from there."

"Jim, if we introduce pieces, as you suggest, we'll be introducing change for the next two years nonstop. I think we should just do it all at once and be done with it, even if it's more painful. That's the best way to introduce change," says Mark.

"How are we going to teach people how to use the system?" asks Amy.

Albert responds. "That's already been planned. In fact everything is ready to go. Our job is to put together the means to get it out onto the computers with as little disruption to business as possible. We are only concerned with the best way to introduce this system to the European offices. Other teams will work on the rollout in the other company locations. What I have down for us to do today is come up with a way to get the software out. How do we let people know about the change and how much downtime will be necessary?"

"Albert, we can't possibly get this software out in a package people will understand in eight weeks," says Mark.

"We've already hashed that out. We talked and talked about that last time. All we have to do is plan the rollout. Everything else has been done. Can't we move forward?" asks Natalie. "I'm sick to death of constantly going over the same things."

Albert answers, "We're really jumping ahead of ourselves. We are not yet ready to make these kinds of decisions. Why don't we figure out what we need to organize for the rollout? Let's make a list of what decisions need to be made without making any today." **(Albert moves away from his structured agenda. He specifies the problem while he asks the group to organize without decision making.)**

"One thing we need to do is figure out which users will get the system first," Ruth says.

"Yeah, and part of that includes the amount of downtime necessary," adds Amy.

People begin adding to the list. Albert writes down everything people say and then he reads it all back to them.

"It looks as if we are going to need to meet more frequently until we get a plan. Can you guys meet again day after tomorrow at the same time? I will put together what we have and e-mail it out," Albert says.

"There's no way I can meet this often," says Jim. "I've got other priorities right now."

"I know it's frustrating to have to be part of this project when you've got so many other things to do. I'm as frustrated as you sound, Jim. But, if we get this project off the ground successfully, things will be better for all of us. If you can't meet that soon, when can you meet?" **(Joins feelings with fact and poses a positive consequence.)**

"Who else out there thinks we're going to spend the next eight weeks spinning our wheels and then the top brass will tell us what to do the way they want it anyway?" asks Amy.

"Amy, tell me about what is really bothering you?" Albert asks. **(Invites Amy to talk.)**

There's a brief silence. Amy finally says, "I've been on these teams before. We talk and talk about the best way to make this change and to get it out to people. Then, we finally come up with something no one really likes, just to get done by the deadline. The rollout happens and then there's downtime and people go nuts. All the ideas we had never get implemented."

"Amy's right," adds Natalie. "I know you're committed to this process, Albert, but what guarantees can you give us that what we suggest will happen? What's even more important, how can we be sure that what we suggest is going to run as smoothly as possible?"

Albert tells them that he cannot make any guarantees. "I hear your concerns. Before I agreed to take on this project, I asked to select the teams. The only guarantee I can give you is that each of you are people I know and trust. You have shown me that you will produce what you say. Our job is to develop a rollout process for the European offices. I challenge you to think about things we can do to make sure that process will be implemented. You don't have to answer that question now. But, I'd like to keep it front and center as we work. How do you all feel about that?" **(Poses a question to resolve the issue but does not ask for resolution. Instead asks for organization around resolution.)**

Everyone agrees to attend to that question as they work. They also agree to meet in two days at the same time.

Analysis

At the beginning of the meeting when Albert stuck to his carefully constructed agenda, he ran into trouble. The group rebelled and got bogged down in the mire of process, trying to answer questions they were not ready to deal with. Frustrations rose. Groups in the Forming Stage often face this problem. Once Albert moved away from his agenda and began helping the group organize itself, he facilitated some forward motion. From there he could implement the SIJR Model.

Specify the Problem. Albert specified that the group was trying to make process decisions it was not yet ready to make. When Albert moved away from his agenda, he could see this problem. Albert also noticed different personalities on the team, namely, Jim has Bold characteristics and so does Natalie. The Technical in Amy is looking for perfection.

Invite Others to Talk. When people complained or made negative comments, Albert invited them to share with genuine curiosity. He encouraged participation and listened to concerns.

Join Feeling with Fact. Because Albert is dealing with Technicals their feelings are often masked in their language and their voice. Albert listened and heard their frustration. He invited Amy to share more about what was really bothering her and by so doing uncovered concerns that characterized a Technical personality and were probably mirrored by other Technicals in the group.

Resolve the Issue. Albert recognized that this meeting could not resolve all the issues. He showed the group, however, that he heard what they were saying, and he challenged them to look for ways to get their process implemented.

Now that Albert has applied the SIJR Model for the European team, he knows he can do so for each of the other four virtual teams. Each team will be different and will require a different approach.

CONCLUSION

Saying it just right within a group is more complicated than saying it just right to one person. Groups require an understanding of the unique characteristics of team development. We saw two instances where groups nearly failed because members ignored the team development process. The design group panicked because one member catapulted the group into tasks that only a group in the Performing Stage could accomplish. In the second situation we observed Karl's group struggling because of membership changes. Longer-term members resisted going backwards and thus left out the new members by developing a strong clique.

Typical problems in groups such as constant lateness, tasks not getting completed, or disagreement and strife among members usually signal a group in the Storming Stage. Leaders of those groups must patiently allow members to organize themselves around the group mission. Bold and Expressive leaders tend to move too quickly from stage to stage, as we saw with Karl. Technicals make good team leaders when they understand the logic of the team development process as we saw with Albert. Technicals have the patience to allow the group to develop in its own way. Sympathetics make good team leaders if they can tolerate the natural strife of the Storming Stage.

Finally, the last situation demonstrated how difficult it is to manage a group you cannot see. Albert had the good sense to select group members. By doing so, he hoped to move more quickly from the Forming and Storming Stages into the Norming and Performing Stages. We saw, however, that even with that precaution, Albert faced a group wishing to jump ahead with tasks only groups in the Performing Stage might tackle. He had to backtrack in order to keep the group moving.

Chapter 8 departs from group sticky situations to an examination of how office relationships affect our ability to *say it just right*. In particular we will explore what options are available to us when sexual harassment becomes an issue.

NOTES

1. Bruce W. Tuckman, *Conducting Educational Research* (New York: Harcourt Brace Jovanovich, 1972).

2. William H. Whyte, *The Organization Man* (New York: Simon & Schuster, 1956).

Chapter 8

Sticky Romantic Situations in the Office

Your boss tells you how attractive you look. You notice two co-workers talking intimately in the coffee shop. You spot your deputy assistant staring at you. Today's workplace is ripe for sticky situations between the sexes. Now that we no longer have a male-dominated workforce, we run into new questions and dilemmas all the time. Perhaps the questions are not so new, but they have taken a new turn. Fifteen to twenty years ago, office romance of any kind was considered taboo. Today, however, according to Bixler and Dugan, there are more office romances than in any other environment. They say office romances are as common as laptops.[1]

What differences exist from the work environment of our parents to the work environment of today? According to the Bureau of Labor Statistics, there are more women in the workplace than ever. "Women's labor force participation rates have increased significantly over the past 50 years, narrowing the gap between rates for women and men."[2]

Furthermore people are more sensitive to the issue of sexual harassment today than in the past. As illustrated in the popular television series *Mad Men*, years ago a woman who might have felt harassed

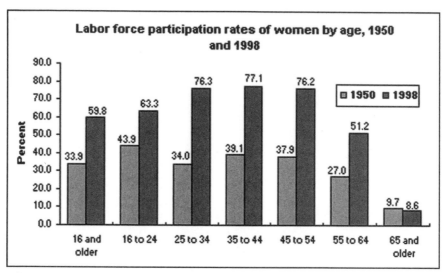

Labor Force Participation Rates of Women by Age, 1950 and 1998

by her boss faced either putting up with it or leaving the job.[3] Finally, in today's world of work the male-female relationship no longer consists of the all powerful male over the weaker female. The playing field is more level. Everything shifted, and those shifts cause us to stop and wonder what to do. We not only encounter a myriad of sticky situations, but we also face the legal ramifications of sexual harassment. A Boston-based consulting firm, Novations Group, reported that 38 percent of female employees heard sexually inappropriate comments at work in 2007, up from 22 percent in 2006.[4] The modern workplace complicates any type of intimate relationship. Whether you are attracted to someone above you, below you, or next to you, you must consider the risks you take when you engage in a romantic relationship at work.

WHAT MAKES TODAY'S WORKPLACE RIPE FOR ROMANCE?

Besides the natural shift in the workplace with more women taking powerful roles in organizations, what else makes our work environment ripe for romance? Bixler and Dugan list several reasons[5] people find office attraction attractive:

1. There are more single, young people in the workplace of both sexes.
2. New opportunities to meet people of similar interests, skills, and tastes are too tempting.

3. We spend most of our waking hours at work. Research shows that most of our friends are people with whom we work. Naturally we might find our soul mate among those friends at work.

4. The workplace is a safe environment for meeting people in contrast to bars or internet encounters.

5. People are thrown together to work on projects. They depend on and trust one anther to carry out tasks. As the proverbial saying goes, one thing leads to another.

6. At work you meet people with similar interests. An attorney who defends the downtrodden lives by certain values as a person. How does that attorney find a partner with similar values? Most likely he or she will run into that ideal person at work. Work puts us next to people similar to us.

STICKY SITUATIONS AND SEXUAL HARASSMENT

The new workplace, where men and women work together in all kinds of situations, begs the question, What does sexual harassment mean? Unfortunately the laws do not always help us understand the answer to this question.

The Federal Equal Employment Opportunity Commission has defined sexual harassment as "unwelcome sexual advances, requests for sexual favors, and other verbal or physical conduct of a sexual nature when submission to or rejection of such conduct is used as the basis for employment decisions . . . or such conduct has the purpose or effect of creating an intimidating, hostile or offensive working environment."[6]

You may read what the law says and ask yourself, how do I know what constitutes an intimidating or hostile environment? The first part of the law clearly states that if you request sexual favors for something in return for something else, or *quid pro quo*, you violate the law. As the following example illustrates, the second part is less straightforward.

> *Phyllis recently ended a relationship with her co-worker, Martin. They had lived together for over a year. When things soured, Phyllis told Martin she wanted to end the relationship, and she asked him to move out. Because they work together, Martin and Phyllis see each other every day. As sales representatives for a large drug company, they travel separately to different territories, but when in the office, they work side by side. Martin did not want to break up the relationship. He vowed he loved Phyllis. Now that the*

affair is over, Phyllis notices that she can't get rid of Martin. He hangs around her desk. He touches her intimately as if they were still involved. She tells him to stop and pushes him away when he tries to kiss her. Martin does not get the message. The last time he came to her office, she told him if he continued to hang out in her cubicle and attempted to kiss her, she would file a sexual harassment complaint. Martin laughed and said, "Who'll believe you. Everyone knows we're an item."

Is Phyllis justified in filing a complaint against Martin? After all, she had been romantically involved with him, and as he said, everyone in the office knew of their affair.

Even so, the law says when behaviors are sexual and unwelcome, as in the case with Phyllis and Martin, sexual harassment exists. If Phyllis wants to file a complaint, she has several choices in terms of levels of severity:

1. Make a strong assertion to Martin. Clearly indicate what behaviors she finds offensive and what she wants him to stop doing.
2. Document the conversations she's had with Martin and document his offensive behaviors. Consult her company's sexual harassment guidelines and talk to her Human Resources manager.
3. If Martin continues to ignore Phyllis, she will have no choice but to take the complaint to her boss.

Sticky situations involving sexual harassment can disrupt the entire operations of a company. One main difficulty with any office relationship is how it makes others feel. You can report sexual harassment even when you were not the target of a sexually harassing behavior. If you witness something and find it offensive, you can file a complaint under the law. Harassment as well as consensual office romances that involve major players in the company and/or married people can have a negative effect on morale.

Determine the Costs

The SIJR Model begins with the *Decision Points*. The first decision point is to *determine the costs*. Before we look at individual situations involving office relationships, let's look at the typical costs involved when deciding whether or not to engage in an office romance.

We all know the risks when we decide to have a relationship with a married person or when we decide to flirt with our boss. What are the costs, however, in a less risky situation, namely, between two single co-workers who work for a large company where they probably won't get fired if they become romantically involved. In this case, perhaps the risks are less obvious than those when the person we're interested in is our superior or a client or a subordinate, but risks still exist.

All relationships carry risk. Being in an office romance multiplies in difficulty because if the relationship ends, you will see the person every day at work (remember Phyllis and Martin). You will run into that individual after he or she starts dating someone else. You will have to deal with your hurt constantly if you stay in your job.

1. Can you control your emotions in your work environment? Romance of any kind at work is inappropriate. Are you okay with seeing the person you are intimate with across the room without going to talk to that person? Are you sacrificing important business dates with others because you want to share time with your partner? Do you feel jealous when your partner interacts with others in the office?

2. How do others in the office respond to your relationship? If you want to keep the intimate relationship secret, how are you dealing with that? It's not a good idea to put your partner down publicly just to pretend you don't care. People see through this kind of behavior. On the other hand, if you are always sticking up for your partner, that, too, looks unprofessional.[7]

3. Being in an office relationship means seeing your partner all day every day with little time to yourself. You work with that person; you go home with that person. When is it too much of a good thing? Many husbands and wives find they cannot work together because they need some distance from each other. We sometimes believe that being with the one we love all the time would be a heavenly situation. This is not always the case and does not mean you love someone less for it. We all need our personal space.

4. When you have a relationship with a co-worker, competitive issues often emerge. How will you feel if your partner gets that promotion you hoped for? Or, what if you get that promotion you know your partner really wanted?

As we examine specific sticky romantic situations, we notice that few absolutes exist. Go into the relationship with a clear understanding of the costs and be willing to make sacrifices if you must. Above all, act professionally.

STICKY SITUATION # 15:
A BOSS WHO FLIRTS

Roberta is the owner and manager of a large global company, Suretel, that produces a small computer chip for buyers like Microsoft and Intel. She launched the company in the 1990s and went public during the dot-com era. Her timing has always been impeccable. She senses when it's right to make certain bold moves, and she never hesitates nor looks back. When Roberta wants something, she goes for it. She's an energetic leader who has always won the respect of her staff and her board. The company is headquartered in San Diego but has offices around the globe. In recent years, Roberta has worked primarily out of the San Diego office side by side with the administrative team of Suretel.

Two years earlier Roberta hired Dave as the CFO for the company. She trusts him implicitly. Dave came to Suretel with high recommendations. He'd worked previously for a large computer company, and he is a CPA. Everything Dave does, he does methodically. Roberta trusts his judgment and relies on him to keep her on course and never steer her astray. Even though he has only been with the company a couple of years, she has confided in others that she has a warm spot for Dave, and she sees him as her partner. She often discusses non-financial matters with him that do not directly affect him, just to get his take on things. Roberta, who never had time for deep romantic relationships, remains single. Dave is married and has two children. Roberta likes Dave's wife and has met his children. Nonetheless, she sees Dave as her "spouse" at work.

Today, while Dave pores over the financial reports at his desk, Roberta comes up behind him and covers his eyes with her hands. Her long hair hangs over his head, "Guess who?" she says. Dave nearly jumps out of his chair. "Roberta, what in the world are you playing at?"

She laughs. "Chill out, Dave. I'm just kidding around." She plops down in the chair across from him. "What are your lunch plans? I'd like to discuss that deal we've been talking about regarding the new branch office."

Dave checks his calendar. He has a lunch date with his wife. They're having a problem with their teenage son and decided to meet for lunch to talk about strategies. "I can't today."

Roberta rises and sits on the side of his desk. She flips her hair over her shoulder and smiles at him. "Come on, Dave, what could be more important than a date with your boss?"

Dave sighs. "Can we talk any other time?" He knows she doesn't really want to talk about the branch office deal. They talked that already nearly to death.

Roberta hops off his desk. "Well, if you must play hard to get," she looks at him under hooded eyes. "Come on, Dave. I've got appointments all week. This is my only free hour. There's no one I'd rather share it with. I'll treat you to a glass of your favorite Pinot."

"You know I never drink during the work day."

Her voice drops. "Not before five. But after that, well, don't make me beg."

Dave agrees to the lunch. He calls his wife and cancels their plans.

During lunch Roberta toys with Dave's foot under the table. She slips off her shoe and touches his leg with her bare toes. She giggles and teases him as if she were his lover. He feels decidedly uncomfortable, but she's a very attractive woman. Her attention and her girlish behavior excite him, especially since he's seen her operate in the boardroom where she's anything but girlish. When she acts like this, she seems more human. Despite himself, Dave laughs at her jokes and listens while she talks about her family and her deepest dreams. But as they amuse one another, he wonders just where this relationship with Roberta is headed.

APPLYING THE SAY IT JUST RIGHT MODEL

DECISION POINTS

Dave weighs the costs. Dave enjoys Roberta's flirtations. Even though she makes him uncomfortable because he's not sure how to respond, he likes the attention. She singles him out to discuss important business decisions. She implicitly trusts him. Dave likes his job. The company is growing and Roberta rewards him with salary bonuses and exotic trips. He's noticed, however, some tension at home. Having to cancel the lunch date with his wife put him in a difficult place where he had to decide between his wife and Roberta. His job, although important, comes second to his marriage. He can find another job if he must. He has good credentials. What worries him more is destroying Roberta's trust. If he talks to her about her flirtatious behavior, she might pull back and extinguish their friendship. Could he continue to work for her if she gives him the cold shoulder? Even more important, would he consider having an affair with her? Because his marriage and family come first, he rejects this option. The thought of having an affair frightens him. But the costs of losing Roberta's trust are also high.

Dave sets his limits. Dave decides that Roberta is going too far. He must tell her that he cannot jeopardize his marriage for his work. Roberta asked him to go on a site visit with her to the offices on the East Coast. During such a trip he anticipates being with her day and night. That opportunity excites him, but he also dreads it. He fears that things might get out of hand. He decides not go on any more overnight trips without first talking to Roberta and setting some limits.

Dave determines the power sources. Dave feels powerless. As boss and owner of the company, Roberta holds all the cards. He cannot report her behavior to anyone, nor does he really want to. He appreciates the attention, but he worries about where it will lead. Dave wants to keep his job, but he knows that if he talks candidly with Roberta, she might overreact. She does not respond well to people whom she considers "traitors." Dave has always tried to stay on her good side. She could retaliate. Because of her reputation in the technology industry, she could damage Dave beyond firing him. From Dave's vantage point, his only source of power lies in playing to her sense of morality and decency. Dave is not only a husband but a father. His role as a father might give him leverage to help Roberta see that there is no future in their relationship.

Personality Overlay

Dave knows that Roberta is a Bold personality. She takes risks easily and does not have time for interpersonal relations. She's spent most of her life building her business which is her first love. Dave characterizes himself as a Technical with some Expressive traits. The Expressive part of him likes the attention Roberta has shown him, but the Technical in him pulls back. He understands that he must listen to his Technical self, which is waving cautionary flags around Roberta's behavior. Sometimes Dave imagines he will succumb to Roberta's enticements and fall into an affair with her. But then the Technical in him warns that such an arrangement spells failure. Roberta has never had a long-term relationship with a man. Dave must make it clear to her in terms a Bold will understand that an intimate relationship for them will destroy their friendship and their ability to work together. For him, it will doom his future with the company and possibly with the industry.

Say It Just Right Conversation

Dave goes to Roberta's office and asks to meet with her at 6 P.M.

"I appreciate your seeing me this evening. I know you're really slammed with the branch deal, but I wanted to clear the air about some things," Dave begins.

Roberta pushes her reading glasses on her head and raises her brows, "Clear the air?"

Dave settles across from Roberta and looks down at the arm of the chair. "I really enjoy working here—"

"My God, you're not quitting are you?" she interrupts.

Dave laughs. "I hope not. But I am feeling uncomfortable. You see. I don't know how to say this so I'm going to just spit it out. I get the impression that you'd like our relationship to be more personal." **(Specifies the problem.)**

Roberta smiles. "Are you suggesting that you feel uncomfortable with me?"

Dave shifts in his seat. "It's not you I'm uncomfortable with, it's the way you sometimes behave. When we went to lunch yesterday, you were acting more like my wife than my boss. That makes me nervous. I like you, and I find you an extremely attractive, appealing woman, but I'm not in a position to go beyond that. I love my wife and family and want to keep that part of my life intact." **(Joins feelings with facts.)**

Roberta shakes her head. "Of course you want to keep your family intact. I never expected anything else from you."

"Look, Roberta, there's no question that there might be something between us. But, I'm not comfortable with exploring that option. I like my job, and I appreciate the trust you put in me. I'd love to have a smooth working relationship without it going beyond what is professional. What is your take on this?" **(Invites her to talk.)**

Roberta leans back in her chair and stretches upward. "I never meant to make you feel nervous and uncomfortable. But, I won't pretend that I don't find you attractive. I'm stimulated by the way you think. It's too bad, well, forget it. I get what you're saying, and I'll behave myself."

"Behaving ourselves is one option, but I also suggest we set some parameters."

She laughs. "That sounds just like you. Okay, what do you suggest?"

"First of all, before you say anything to me, ask yourself if you'd say that if my wife were in the room. I will do the same thing. We can keep each other in check that way. Secondly, I suggest we do not travel together, at least for a while. That means I won't be able to take that trip to Boston next month. I'm sure Jennifer would love the opportunity to go. How do you feel about these ideas?" (**Looks for resolution.**)

A frown crosses Roberta's face. "I don't mind the 'wife' test. But, I need you on that Boston trip. We've got to talk about how to approach the downsizing on the East Coast. Jennifer can't do that. Maybe we could go separately. I'll leave two days ahead of you. We could also stay in two different hotels."

"But we'll be eating dinner together every night," says Dave with a sigh.

"Not necessarily. My cousin lives nearby. I'll go see her and spend some time there. That will give you several days on your own."

"Okay. That might work." He pauses. "You've heard a couple of my parameters. What parameters might you suggest?"

Roberta shrugs. "Well, maybe we need to limit our contacts at the office. I probably drop by your area too frequently. How about we work out a regular meeting three times each week?"

Dave grins. "Is that something you really think you can do?"

"Let's give it a shot."

"Okay. How about first thing in the morning, Monday, Wednesday, and Friday?"

"That works. Anything else?"

"That's it for now. Thanks for listening to me and for helping me resolve this issue. I want to keep working here. I'd hate for anything between us to jeopardize that." He rises to leave.

"Ditto there," Roberta says.

ANALYSIS

There is no guarantee that Roberta will change her behavior. But Dave can, at least, point out when she crosses the line. Because he was dealing with a Bold, he had to get directly to the point, and he had to be careful not to respond to a "quick fix." When Roberta said she'd behave, she thought the matter was finished. Dave pushed harder to come to a resolution he thought might stick.

Specify the Problem. The problem was that Dave felt Roberta wanted more from him than a professional relationship. He did not delay in saying this, and he said it as directly as he could. With a Sympathetic or an Expressive, he might have had to give Roberta more strokes and eased himself into the discussion. Roberta's Bold personality enabled him to get to the point quickly.

Invite the Other Person to Talk. Dave did not invite Roberta to talk right away. He waited until he had fully expressed what he thought was going on. He did that because he was dealing with a Bold personality. Had he invited her to talk too soon, she may have dismissed the problem. Instead he made it clear how he felt and what the consequences might be then he invited her to share her "take" on the problem.

Join Feeling with Fact. Dave talked about feeling uncomfortable and nervous. He made it clear that it was Roberta's behaviors that made him uncomfortable, not Roberta herself. He, thereby, let Roberta know that his unease could change.

Resolve the Issue. Dave pushed for a resolution he could live with. Feeling uncomfortable traveling with Roberta, he gave her an opportunity to come up with a plan for travel that would satisfy him. He also asked her for other things they could do to set parameters on their relationship.

STICKY SITUATION #16:
ROMANCE THAT DISRUPTS THE OFFICE

Dr. Jordan is the surgical director for a large regional hospital. The department employs 14 physicians as well as a broad complement of aides, nurses, physicians' assistants, and other staff. Last year one of the senior surgeons, Larry Stewart, and a new surgeon, Roxanne Mosley, started an affair. This relationship became apparent to Dr. Jordan after finding the two physicians in a compromising position in the doctor's lounge. At that time, Dr. Jordan asked them to be more discreet, but he did not take further action.

In recent months, the relationship has caused some difficulty among the staff. Larry Stewart is married to a woman who runs the hospital's development program. Everyone knows and likes Larry's wife, Nancy. Before the affair with Roxanne Mosley, Larry and Nancy ate lunch frequently in the hospital cafeteria where other staff interacted with the couple. Furthermore, one of Nancy's best friends, Margaret James, works as a physician's assistant in the department. She makes her disapproval of the relationship known by saying several nasty things to Roxanne in hearing range of patients.

Recently Dr. Jordan learned that rumors of the affair had reached the hospital administrator through a board member.

APPLYING THE SAY IT JUST RIGHT MODEL

DECISION POINTS

Dr. Jordan weighs the costs. The affair between Drs. Stewart and Mosley is causing problems in the department. He catches people talking about the couple in the corridors of the department. The two "lovers" can't seem to keep away from one another. During meetings they sit together and use any excuse to touch one another. They also support each other's comments without censure. Dr. Stewart has been with the department for a long time, and everyone respects him as a surgeon. Dr. Mosley is newer, but she's highly skilled. Dr. Jordan would hate to lose either one of these gifted physicians, but if he does nothing, he fears that the affair will tear the entire department apart. Some people side with the couple while others side against them.

Dr. Jordan sets limits. Dr. Jordan does not really care about what people do in their personal lives so long as that behavior does not affect the operations of the department. He decides that Drs. Stewart and Mosley must decide if they are going to continue their relationship and if so, one or both must resign.

Determines the power sources. Even though Dr. Jordan feels confident that he has a strong power base, he recognizes that Dr. Stewart carries a lot of weight based on his outstanding reputation as a surgeon. Jordan expects that the hospital administrator will fight for keeping Stewart. Fewer people know Mosley, but her skill has become recognized. Dr. Jordan feels he must take action even if it means a battle with the hospital administration and perhaps some board members. He feels if it comes to them or him, he will survive.

PERSONALITY OVERLAY

We do not have very much information about the personalities of the two lovers. We suspect surgeons, however, have a high dose of Technical in their personalities. The risk Dr. Stewart is taking by openly having an affair with a colleague, suggests some Bold in him and perhaps some Expressive. Dr. Mosley is taking less risk. Her personality is more difficult to determine. Dr. Jordan delayed taking action when he first learned of the affair. This caution suggests a Technical personality.

SAY IT JUST RIGHT CONVERSATION

"I called you two into my office to talk to you about a matter that concerns me. It's no secret that the two of you are involved in a romantic relationship." (**Specifies the problem immediately.**)

Stewart sits up. "Whose business is that of anyone's?"

"Unfortunately, it has become the business of the hospital. I've had complaints from staff within our department, and I recently heard a comment from a board member. I'm distressed that this behavior reflects badly on our department. Already I see morale dropping. I'm curious to know what ideas you might have to resolve this problem." (**Invites them to talk.**)

Mosley sighs. "I think people should focus on doing their jobs and leave us alone. That's in the best interest of the patients and the hospital."

"Of course it is," said Stewart. "What we do affects no one but us."

"That's where you're wrong. Because both of you are highly respected physicians in this department, it affects everyone. Larry, I'm not judging you, but your wife works on the fourth floor. How long before she hears about this? I'm worried that she could cause major problems for our division." (**Joins feelings with facts.**)

"Leave her to me."

"What would you have us do?" Mosley asks. "Resign?"

Dr. Jordan fiddles with his pen. "I'm not asking either of you to resign just yet. I'm interested in learning what you think can be done to resolve this problem." (**Persists in inviting them to help**

with the resolution without denying the possible consequence of resignation.)

Stewart reaches over and takes Mosley's hand. "If Roxanne resigns, I will, too."

Dr. Jordan takes a deep breath. "I'm frustrated and disappointed that you are unwilling to come up with a solution other than resignation." (**Joins feelings with facts.**)

"Well, we're not going to end our relationship just because a bunch of gossipy people aren't happy with it," says Stewart.

"Besides resigning and ending your relationship, what else might you do?" Dr. Jordan asks.

Mosley says. "I guess we could work different shifts. That way we won't be running into each other all the time."

Dr. Jordan nods. "What else?"

"I'm going to talk to Nancy," Stewart resolves. "I've been meaning to do that, but—well, I guess I haven't wanted to hurt her."

"She'll be hurt more when she finds out about the relationship through the grapevine," Dr. Jordan says and adds, "Is there anything else the two of you could do?" (**Pushes to get them to resolve the issue.**)

They are silent.

Jordan continues. "You need to be more discreet when you're together. It doesn't help matters when people find you kissing in the hallways or holding hands in the doctor's lounge." He pauses. "As I see it, one of you needs to move out of this department. Even if you follow through on everything you've suggested today, the situation has become too volatile. Once you've figured out who wants to move, let me know. I'll do everything I can to help you find a suitable position either in this hospital or elsewhere. You are both excellent physicians. I do not want to lose either of you, but I have little choice. My hope is we can keep one of you." (**Looking for resolution.**)

Mosley says, "I know Larry said he'd leave if I left, but I don't think that's a good idea. I've already been looking, and it would be a lot easier for me to go someplace else."

Dr. Jordan concludes, "So, you're going to begin working different shifts. Larry, you're going to come clean with Nancy. The two of you are going to stop being so overt with your feelings in public, and finally, Roxanne you're going to search for a new position. Is there anything else?" (**Summarizes the resolution.**)

Both agree to what they've discussed. "Again, Roxanne, I'll do everything I can to help you locate a new position. I'm sure this will all work out with time," says Dr. Jordan.

ANALYSIS

Of course, Dr. Jordan cannot force Roxanne and Larry to be more discreet. He cannot make them curtail their acts of affection in public. But, he can adjust the schedule to enable them to work different shifts. He can also do everything in his power to transfer Roxanne to another department or hospital.

Furthermore, during the SIJR Conversation, Dr. Jordan carefully avoided being judgmental with either party, particularly with Dr. Stewart. He simply told him what might happen if he did not confess to his wife. He didn't say it was right to talk to her and wrong to have an affair. Both Stewart and Mosley were defensive enough without making accusations. Technicals tend to be judgmental. It took all Dr. Jordan's strength of character to refrain from his natural tendency to judge. In so doing, he got them past their defensiveness and focused on trying to resolve the problem in a professional manner. He pushed them to come up with solutions they could abide.

Specify the Problem. Being a Technical, Jordan had little difficulty quickly specifying the problem in clear, unemotional terms. Both doctors, particularly Dr. Stewart, responded defensively right away. Dr. Jordan expected that response. He did not, however, want Stewart's defensiveness to escalate into anger.

Invite Others to Talk. When Dr. Jordan asked them what would resolve the problem, he invited them to share solutions with him. He did not ask them to talk about their relationship. He wanted them to focus on the future and come up with a solution. He had to push them by inviting them to talk about solutions several times. At first they could only see the obvious solutions, namely, leave or end the affair. It wasn't until they became less defensive that they opened their eyes to other options to resolve the problem.

Join Feeling with Fact. Dr. Jordan joined feeling with fact when he talked to Dr. Stewart about opening up to his wife. He also shared his frustration when the couple continued to respond defensively without sharing ideas for resolution.

Resolve the Issue. Once the couple suggested ideas that could resolve the problem, Dr. Jordan listened and waited until the end of the SIJR Conversation before he tossed in his ideas.

STICKY SITUATION #17:
YOU FIND YOUR SUBORDINATE HOT

Calvin hired Melissa five months ago. He liked her immediately. During the interview they talked freely as if they'd known each other for years. She made him laugh. He appreciated her quick humor. He hired her without hesitation to serve as the sales manager over a challenging territory. Her experience in sales suggested she'd bring a fresh approach to the business. She's performed beyond expectations. Not only did she reestablish ties that had been threatened, but she also brought in new business. He suspects that he's not alone in appreciating her easy manner and fresh appearance.

Recently Calvin discovered himself thinking about Melissa at odd times during the day. When she's traveling, he wonders where she is and what she's doing and is anxious for her return. Usually he allows the sales team to work independently with periodic updates. But, whenever Melissa returns from a trip, he calls her into his office on the pretext of wanting an update on results from the meetings. She seems relaxed and easy about these encounters, but he knows he's stepping over the line. What concerns him even more is he's been dreaming about Melissa and has awakened from those dreams very aroused. He worries that the situation might get out of hand, and he's not sure where to take it.

APPLYING THE SAY IT JUST RIGHT MODEL

DECISION POINTS

Calvin weighs the costs. Melissa is single, and so is Calvin. He knows that she is not seeing someone at the moment. He came out of a long-term relationship a few months back. Calvin feels a spark between him and Melissa and suspects that something special might be there. On the other hand, if Calvin approaches her in a personal way, he will lose her as an employee. She's performed very well for his division, and he expects that they will all benefit with extra bonuses this year. She's turned around an otherwise very difficult territory. Losing her would be difficult for him to explain to his boss. If they decide to date and it does not work out, he's lost a very good employee and still he's alone. But, if he they decide to test their interest in one another and it works out, he may have found his soul mate. The costs are high either way.

Calvin sets limits. Calvin does not want to lose Melissa, but he does want to know if she welcomes his feelings. He decides that he cannot go on wondering. He must risk offending her in order to learn how she feels about him. If they share a mutual attraction, the two of them can talk about future steps together instead of him making this decision alone.

Calvin determines the power sources. Even though Calvin is Melissa's boss, he does not see himself in a very powerful place. She is an excellent employee who can find a job anywhere. If things do not work out between them and she wishes to leave, he would gladly give her high recommendations. He, on the other hand, has a lot to lose. His boss was relieved when they hired Melissa and quite pleased with her results. He will not be happy if she resigns because Calvin has taken a shine to her.

PERSONALITY OVERLAY

Calvin is a cautious and sensitive person. He's not a Bold and likely not an Expressive. The cautious part of him is holding back his feelings and the sensitive part of him wants to know how Melissa feels. Based on these behaviors, he is probably a Sympathetic with a high Technical backup style.

Melissa, on the other hand, is friendly, outgoing, and easy to be with. She quickly turned around a very difficult territory. Her easy manner and quick wit suggest she's an Expressive personality.

Recognizing that Melissa is an Expressive, Calvin can approach her without necessarily losing her as an employee or as a friend because Expressives appreciate attention. Technical personality types might have trouble remaining in a job when the boss is physically attracted to them because they tend to make feelings logical and consider those feelings dangers to their careers. A Sympathetic might be so concerned with how Calvin feels that she'd have trouble turning him down. She'd likely construct barriers between them to enable her to do her job but feel as if she were constantly hurting him. Her ultimate decision would be to leave the company. A Bold personality would be annoyed with Calvin, perhaps even angry with him. If the Bold did not share Calvin's feelings, she'd see him as a threat to her progress in the company and either leave or file a harassment claim.

SAY IT JUST RIGHT CONVERSATION

Calvin and Melissa sit down together after one of her sales trips. She's grown accustomed to him wanting to see her as soon as she returns. They've just finished talking about how the trip went.

"You've really done an outstanding job with that territory," Calvin says. "When we hired you, we told you not to expect results too soon because we've had trouble there for so long. But, you've proven everyone wrong. Congratulations."

Melissa smiles and nods. "It wasn't as bad as you all thought. All I had to do was play nice and listen to a few complaints. There was just one contract that I worried about and even they came around after a bit. Your support and guidance really helped me."

Calvin looks down at his hands. "Actually, Melissa, that's not what I really wanted to talk about." He shifts in his seat. "You see, I've, well, I'm not sure how to say this," he pauses. "I'm frustrated with myself because, well, I've had these feelings for you. I know I shouldn't because you work for me, but I haven't been able to stop myself. I think about you a lot more than I should." He glances at her to determine her reaction. (**Specifies the problem.**)

She studies him with wide eyes and a small smile. At least she hasn't recoiled, he thinks. "Anyway," he adds, "My feelings have gotten stronger, and I'm worried I might say or do something to offend you. So, I felt I had better come clean and see what we might do about it. Could you help me out here?" he says with a shy chuckle. (**Joins feelings with facts. Invites her to talk.**)

"I appreciate your telling me this. I suspected as much." She looks away briefly. "I can't say that I don't find you attractive. One of the reasons I took this job was you. On the other hand, I really like this job. It's exactly what I love doing. I'd hate to jeopardize it."

Calvin lets out a breath. "You probably also know we'd hate to lose you. I'm curious to hear how we might manage this situation and still continue to work together." (**Invites her to talk.**)

After a brief silence, Melissa says, "Maybe we could take it slowly. You know, go out to dinner and get to know one another that way. Then if things seem to get serious, I'll start thinking about looking for another job." (**Resolving the situation.**)

"You sound so sad when you say that," he says. "I don't want you to leave the company any more than you do. I'm sure we could transfer you to another division. You know how much Mr. Peterson values your work." (**Shows compassion for her.**)

"But, I really like sales. I'm not sure I'd be happy in another division."

Calvin straightens up in his chair. "I sense that leaving would distress you a great deal. That is something I really don't want to be responsible for."

She turns toward him. "But if we are really right for each other, it would be worth it. I'm willing to take the risk if you are."

He laughs. "Who could turn that down?" He adds, "You know, of course, you don't have to leave. Who knows, I might find something else." He pauses. "Let's just see where things take us. There are plenty of other options. I could see you working in the marketing and promotions division. That would be a logical step anyway, and it would mean less travel. I'd like that," he says with a laugh. (**Suggests other resolutions.**)

Melissa raises her brows. "Yes, that might be a good option. So long as I can work with people. I'd hate to be shut away in front of a computer all day, that's all. And, actually, I enjoy the travel. But, I must admit, it has been a bit much. My cat misses me a lot." (**Responding to the idea of change.**)

They both laugh. "So," he says, "how about dinner tomorrow night?"

"Let's wait until the weekend. I want to give all this a bit more thought. I can't quite get used to the idea of dating you."

They agree.

ANALYSIS

It took great courage for Calvin to broach Melissa the way he did. Not being a Bold, he had trouble getting right to the matter. Once he did, however, he clearly told her how he felt. He put the burden of the situation on himself. She responded positively. He invited her to talk on several occasions. As the conversation went on she seemed to soften to the idea and showed a willingness to take the risks. Calvin's goal was to share his feelings and determine how she felt. He accomplished that. He did not want to lose her in his division, but he recognized that if their relationship turned romantic, their work situation would need to change. Being a Sympathetic, he listened to her feelings and was ready to do whatever it took to make her comfortable.

At the end of the conversation, he risked asking her to dinner, but she put him off. It made sense for her to want to give the idea of dating her boss more thought.

Specify the Problem. Calvin not only shared how he felt about Melissa, but he also specified that he worried about being inappropriate or unprofessional if he didn't tell her how he felt. That was the real problem.

Invite the Other Person to Talk. Calvin asked Melissa to talk immediately. He wanted to hear her feelings which, as an Expressive, she had no trouble sharing.

Join Feelings with Facts. Calvin allowed himself to open up and share his feelings, but he did so by critically examining the facts. He clearly stated that if they became involved, their work situation would have to change. He let her know, however, how much he and his boss valued her work.

Resolve the Issue. Melissa came up with the solution to move slowly. She seemed to warm to the idea as the conversation progressed. When she thought about leaving her job, she became sad, but after thinking more, she decided she could work elsewhere and be happy. She made the decision to take the risk. Calvin had already made that decision by talking to her in the first place.

Conclusion

When dealing with sticky romantic situations, many issues come into play. In the first case we saw that Dave decided to gently rebuff the romantic overtures by Roberta. Even though Dave found Roberta attractive and her flirtations stimulating, he chose not to take the huge risks of losing his family and his job by getting romantically involved with his boss.

The second situation involved two people whose relationship affected the work of others. Dr. Jordan could not let the couple destroy morale or cause problems up the line. He spoke to them in a nonjudgmental but clear manner, stipulating that one of them must leave in order to prevent further erosion in the department. Saying it just right enabled the couple to drop their defenses and to make a decision that would satisfy all parties.

The final situation involved an unmarried superior who was attracted to an unmarried subordinate. In this situation, the couple had to look at the risks together to decide a course of action they could both accept. By saying it just right, Calvin expressed his feelings and maintained his professionalism.

In the next chapter we look at sticky situations that happen during the interview process. Interviewing for a job is one of the most difficult things any of us must do. As we put ourselves out there for others to judge, we become the commodity for sale. Candidates for jobs often find themselves in very vulnerable positions. When sticky interview situations arise, being able to *say it just right* gets tougher.

NOTES

1. Susan Bixler and Lisa Scherrer Dugan, *5 Steps to Professional Presence: How to Project Confidence, Competence, and Credibility at Work* (Avon, MA: Adams Media Corporations, 2001), 159.

2. Bureau of Labor Statistics, February 2000.

3. Mad Men, AMCtv.com, www.amctv.com/originals/madmen.

4. Rachel Pomerance, "You Want a Piece of Me?" *Pink Magazine*, July–August 2008: 61.

5. Bixler and Dugan, 158–61.

6. "The U.S. Equal Employment Opportunity Commission, Facts About Sexual Harassment," http://law.frecadvice.com/resources/gov_material/eeoc_sexual_harassment_facts.htm.

7. Bixler and Dugan, 162.

Chapter 9

Sticky Interview Situations

Employment Interviews abound with sticky situations. For the candidate the interview is one of the hardest places to be. Candidates must "sell" themselves to the interviewer. They must put themselves on the line for someone else to judge. It has to be one of the most uncomfortable tasks any of us faces in our work lives. The turndowns feel as if someone personally rejected us. For the interviewer, it is not an easy task either. Interviewers do not like to hold someone's future in their hands. For many people, this place also feels awkward and uncomfortable.

In my previous book, *Strategic Interviewing: Skills and Tactics for Savvy Executives*,[1] I introduced a communication strategy for interviewers that makes the decision-making role less subjective. This strategy centers on the POINT selection process (see sidebar). The POINT process gives interviewers the skills they need to make purposeful hiring decisions.

THE POINT SELECTION PROCESS

P   **Plan** the interview.
O   Make the interview **Open**.
IN   Use **INtentional listening** skills to conduct the interview.
T   **Test** the candidate in terms of qualifications. Test the process in terms of openness. Test the fit, regarding the candidate and the job. Test the quality of the interviewer's skills.

WHAT IS A STRATEGIC INTERVIEW?

Strategic interviewing is a system of behavior-based interviewing that strips away the superficial to get at the truth. In essence, a strategic interview by its very nature goes deeper in an attempt to get beyond the surface.

THE PAST

Let's look at the history of the interview. In the past managers interviewed casually and with little preparation. As a result they spent most of the appointment time talking. These early interviews were called *laissez-faire*, a word that comes from the French. It means, "let it be." *Laissez-faire* interviews were conversational in nature. Unfortunately, these kinds of interviews revealed almost nothing about the candidate and gave the interviewer little to go on when making hiring decisions.

Increased turnover alerted those doing the hiring that *laissez-faire* interviewing did not work. In response to this spike in turnover, interviewers strengthened the interview process by giving birth to the structured interview, which consisted of a series of questions asked of each candidate. The goal of the structured interview was to provide structure wherever possible. That meant requiring candidates to have certain basic skills, asking certain questions of all candidates, and scoring candidates in certain consistent ways. There was so much structure that the interviewer lost all opportunity for judgment. Gut-level decision making that can sometimes result in a good hire disappeared.

Recently scientists have learned that gut-level decision making not only exists but also that it is scientifically sound. Daniel Goleman wrote in his book *Primal Leadership*, "the emotional brain activates circuitry that runs from the limbic centers (in the brain) into the gut (sympathetic nervous system), giving us the compelling sense that something feels right." He went on to say, "Gut feeling, in fact, has gained new scientific respect because of recent discoveries about implicit learning—that is, the lessons in life we pick up without being aware we're learning them."[2]

In our reaction against *laissez-faire* interviewing toward structured interviewing, we lost that all-important intuitive part of the interview process. Strategic interviewing enables us to recapture our gut reactions but without the looseness of the *laissez-faire* conversation. Furthermore, it employs focus and parameters more consistent with a structured interview. In other words, strategic interviews blend the best of both styles and produce the best results.

CHARACTERISTICS OF A STRATEGIC INTERVIEW

- Strategic interviews feel **conversational.** One goal of the strategic interview is to help candidates relax so they will tell you something they had not intended to tell you. In so doing, the interviewer engages the candidate in a real conversation. This does not mean the interviewer talks too much, but it does mean the interviewer shares openly. Honesty provokes openness on both sides.

- Strategic interviews focus on the **individual** candidate. If you ask a question you could ask **any** candidate anywhere or you find yourself asking all candidates the same questions, you've missed the essence of being strategic.

- Strategic interviews are **not structured,** but they have a purpose. The purpose depends on the job at hand. As a strategic interviewer, you must determine what skills you are looking for. Questions that deviate from the skills you are searching for are not strategic.

- Everything you do in a strategic interview has **intent.** You have a reason, for example, for asking a closed question. Perhaps you want specific information or you want to quiet a talkative candidate. If you ask a candidate about his or her behavior while playing a team sport, you might want to ascertain how that person works in teams.

- Strategic interviews blend **behavior-based** techniques. Behavior-based questions focus on a candidate's past behavior. Responses based on what the candidate predicts or believes he or she will do at some point in the future give the interviewer little information. Behavior-based interviewing assumes that the best predictor of a person's behavior is the way that person has behaved in the past.

The subsequent sticky interview situations demonstrate not only how to *say it just right* but also what happens when interviewers do not practice strategic interviewing.

STICKY SITUATION #18:
THE CANDIDATE DOESN'T TALK

Paul runs a small novelty business that specializes in collectables. His wife sometimes helps in the store, but she has a full-time job and can no longer fill in. Paul decides he must hire an assistant clerk. After putting an ad in the local paper, he received a dozen inquires. Most of the people who applied had no retail experience and little experience in customer service with the exception of one response which intrigued Paul. That candidate said he had never worked in a store like Paul's, but he had worked in an antique store in the mountains. Paul e-mailed him, and they arranged an interview.

"Good afternoon," Paul says. "Have a seat. May I call you Richard?"

"That's fine."

Paul begins: "I appreciate your applying for this job. I've had the store for almost 10 years and have been operating it on my own with some part-time help from my wife. Recently, however, my wife can't fill in, and I realize that I can't do it all myself. That's why I placed the ad."

"I see."

Paul shifts through the papers on his desk. "I understand you worked in retail before. Tell me what that was like for you."

"I enjoyed it."

"What did you enjoy the most about retail work?"

The candidate shrugs. "The people."

"The people are great," Paul agrees, "but they can also be a challenge. I remember once when I had a woman really scream at me because I didn't have one of the Charles Dickens's collectable houses that she particularly wanted. How have you handled situations like that with customers?"

"I'm not sure I have."

Paul sighs. "It was a bad scene because there were other people in the store. I tried to get her to come with me to the back *where we could talk, but she'd gotten hysterical by then. Can you imagine?"*

The candidate shakes his head and crosses his hands in his lap.

"Tell me about your work in the antique store. What exactly did you do?"

"This and that."

"Did you work full time?"

"Only the weekends."

Paul frowns. "Ah, you worked weekends for a year, right?"

"Yeah."

"I also see," Paul continues, deciding to change the subject, "that you are not from this area. What brought you to our city?"

"School."

"So, you attended the university?"

"No, the Tech School."

"What was that like for you?"

"Good."

By now Paul is sweating. He can't seem to get this candidate to talk. No matter what he asks, the candidate responds in three words or less. Paul cannot imagine him working well with his customers.

Applying the Say It Just Right Model

Decision Points

Paul weighs the costs. The candidate's background looked promising because he had some retail experience. But, Paul's initial impression is not good. He cannot see this candidate working well with people and wonders why he even applied for a job at Paul's store. Rather than give up completely, Paul decides to probe a little further. Paul may have trouble finding a candidate with experience who would want to work as an assistant clerk. Yet, he would rather have someone he can train than an employee who is so impersonal. At the same time, Paul wants to conduct a courteous, professional interview. He does not wish the conversation to end abruptly.

Paul sets his limits. Paul decides to ask questions to try and get the candidate to open up. If the candidate still remains closed, he will end the interview on as polite a note as he can.

Paul determines the power sources. Being in the position to hire, Paul is in the seat of power. He can decide to hire this person or not.

On the other hand, Paul did not get too many promising résumés from his ad, and ads cost a lot. He hates having to start over. Nonetheless, he decides he must invest in more searching rather than hire someone not suited to the job.

Personality Overlay

Paul has trouble determining Richard's personality style. He knows he is not an Expressive because of his reluctance to talk. Even though Paul is not looking to hire an Expressive, necessarily, he is looking for someone who has Expressive tendencies. Expressives love working with people. Paul doubts he is a Sympathetic. Sympathetics would have been more sensitive to Paul's discomfort during the interview. This candidate could be a Bold because his answers are so abrupt. He could also be a Technical because of his cautious responses.

If the candidate is a Bold, Paul might get him to open up with questions that draw out his competitive spirit or his thirst for adventure. If the candidate is a Technical, that approach will not work. A Technical would more likely respond to questions that showcase his organizational skills.

Say It Just Right Conversation

Paul asks, "Richard, you tell me you like working with people, but you've given me no examples of your work with people. What examples do you have?"

Richard shrugs. "I suppose working in the store."

"How did you approach customers in the store?"

"I usually greeted them and asked if I could help them."

Paul continues. "How is that different from the way anyone else might greet a customer?"

Richard takes a breath. "What do you mean?"

"Well, if you enjoy working with people and the only way you tell me you approach people is with the typical, 'Hello. How can I help you?' I see nothing new there. I'm curious to know what's special about your approach." (**Paul tries to touch on his competitive spirit.**)

Richard scratches his head. "I don't really think I have a special approach. I'd just rather work in a store than filing papers somewhere."

"Have you worked filing papers?"

"No, but I don't think I'd like that."

Paul nods. "We have a very special kind of customer here. Most are regulars. They come looking for particular collectables. They're pretty savvy. They search the Web before they come here and know what's available and the price range. Tell me about times you've approached savvy buyers like that."

Richard says, "I usually try and know more than the customer. I would research the products and learn as much as I can about them." **(This response suggests that Richard is a Technical.)**

"It doesn't sound as if what I'm asking is something you've done before."

Richard shakes his head. "I guess not."

"I'm looking for someone who has retail experience and a thirst for helping very savvy customers. I don't really see that you've had that kind of experience." **(Specifies the problem.)**

"Not really. But, I have worked with customers in the store in the mountains."

"I see that. I have to tell you, Richard, I'm a bit confused because I see you've worked in retail, but you've given me no indication that you really like interacting with people and no examples. I sense that you might enjoy researching products. What can you tell me that might suggest something different?" **(Joins feeling with fact and invites Richard to talk.)**

"I tend to be a person of few words."

"My customers are talkers. Some come in just to visit. Many are people I've worked with since I opened the shop. The almost 'family' nature of the business is something they have grown to expect. I'm afraid this job may not be what you were looking for." **(Resolves the problem.)**

"I can see that now." Richard rises to leave.

Paul shakes his hand. "I'm glad you came in. I hope you find the kind of position you are searching for. Good luck to you."

ANALYSIS

Paul kept his interview strategic and behavior-based, even though he recognized that Richard was poorly suited for his job. No matter what approach he used Richard did not open up. Paul asked open questions in a search for examples in Richard's history that might match his job. He explored how Richard approached customers, and he pushed Richard to describe how his approach differed from someone else's. As he went through the interview, he helped Richard recognize that this job might not be a fit for him.

Specify the Problem. Paul clearly described his customer base. He probed Richard for examples of working with that special customer. When Richard answered in the conditional tense, Paul pointed out the obvious, namely, Richard did not have any experience with these customers.

Invite the Other Person to Talk. Paul asked many powerful, open questions that showed a genuine curiosity. These open questions invited Richard to talk, but Richard responded with few words.

Join Feeling with Fact. When Paul said, "I'm a bit confused because you say you've worked in retail . . . " he told Richard that his answers did not jibe with what he said he'd done. He suggested that Richard would enjoy a more solitary job, like researching products; Richard could not deny this observation.

Resolve the Issue. Paul wanted to end the interview in a professional manner. In a job interview, the hiring person can resolve the issue right away or say something like, "We'll be in touch." Paul helped Richard see that this job was not a good fit for him, and he ended the interview with resolution and politeness.

How Strategic an Interviewer Are You?

Answer True or False

1. It's important for your questions to focus on a person's future goals.
2. Interviewers should talk about 50 percent of the time and candidates about 50 percent of the time.
3. You can find out a person's basic philosophy during an interview.
4. Your questions should be tailored just for the person in front of you, not any person who applies for the job.
5. It's okay to ask candidates where they are from.
6. When a job requires certain physical skills, it's okay to ask candidates if they have any physical handicaps that might prevent them from doing the job.
7. You should never ask closed questions in an interview.
8. If a candidate strikes you as unsuitable in the first few seconds of the interview, you should probably reject that candidate in the end.

9. Your planning time before an interview should be three times as much as the interview itself.

10. It's a good idea to ask tough questions to see how a candidate handles pressure.

For your score, look in Appendix 1.

STICKY SITUATION #19:
THE INTERVIEWER WHO CROSSES THE LINE

Wanda recently completed her PhD in chemistry. She's applying for a laboratory job in the research division of a large manufacturing company.

The interviewer begins: "I appreciate your taking the time to visit with me today. My name is Janice Walker. I handle human resources for our division. I'm going to spend the next few minutes trying to get to know you better. What do you like to do in your spare time?"

"I haven't had much spare time. Working on my PhD took every minute. Plus I have two young children. My husband works for a large company that has divisions all over the country. He has to travel a lot. So usually I'm either taking care of the kids or doing my school work."

"Sounds as if you're practically a single parent," Janice says. Wanda laughs, "You could say that."

"And your children take up all your spare time?"

"Yeah, but I don't mind doing stuff around the house, like laundry and cleaning. Those kinds of tasks take my mind off the laboratory work I might be involved in or the teaching assignment I might have for the semester. But the kids do take up a lot of time."

"How do you manage your time between your home responsibilities and your work?" Janice asks.

Wanda takes a deep breath. "That takes a level of maturity. Sometimes you just have to do what you have to do. If a child gets sick, that takes priority. Even though my work is important, nothing is more important than my children and the quality of their lives. My husband and I agree on that. Most of the time, I can arrange my schedule to meet the needs of my family without sacrificing my professional goals. I went to graduate school late; I was 35 when I started. At nearly 40, I now feel I'm more mature than the typical student and that's helped me deal with the stresses at home and at work."

"So you believe your age helps you deal with the pressures your home and work put on you?"

"Now I wouldn't go that far," Wanda says. "It's hard juggling everything. But I love both my role as a parent and my work. At work I love the creative challenge that research offers, and when something exciting happens, well . . . that makes it all worthwhile. The constant interruptions either at work from research assistants or at home from the kids do sometimes wear me down." She pauses. "I wonder if I could talk a few moments about my work in the lab?"

Janice nods. "I was coming to that. But first, you said your children come first. What would you do if you had a crisis with a child but we needed you here at work?" (This is an illegal question because it is probing child care. It is also a nonstrategic question because it focuses on a hypothetical situation in the future instead of behaviors in the past.)

"That's a hard question to answer because it depends on what the crisis might be and what arrangements could be made at work. As I said, my husband travels, but he's not gone all the time. I could call on him if I had to be at the lab."

"Let's say you had to deliver an important presentation to the CEO that day."

"Again, this is hypothetical," Wanda says. "But, I'm sure if I had such an important presentation, I'd make certain the kids were dealt with. In fact, when I had to defend my dissertation, I arranged schedules so my husband was available to manage the kids if anything came up. I tend to take care of everything I can ahead of time."

APPLYING THE SAY IT JUST RIGHT MODEL

DECISION POINTS

Wanda weighs the costs. This interview is making Wanda uncomfortable. Janice is asking many questions related to Wanda's role as a mom. Wanda knows these questions cross the line with regard to their legality. She realizes if she refuses to answer the questions, it will destroy her chances to go further in the interview process. If the Human Resources interview goes well, she'll move on to talk to scientists in the division. But, if she doesn't get past this hurdle, she'll never get that opportunity. The costs are high for her. She can get a job with another company, but this firm offers the best benefits and the best chances for promotion.

Wanda sets limits. Wanda has gently asked the interviewer to focus on her professional knowledge and experience, but the interviewer dismissed this request. She decides that she will continue to steer the interviewer away from the more personal side of her life. If she cannot do so, however, she will point out to Janice that the questions make her uncomfortable.

Wanda determines the power sources. Wanda realizes that the interviewer holds the power. Human resources decide who will pass on to the next phase of interviews and who will not. Nonetheless, Wanda's research project is uniquely suited to this manufacturing industry. She recognizes that she has a lot to offer this company that another candidate might not. That knowledge gives her the confidence to *say it just right* if she must.

SAY IT JUST RIGHT CONVERSATION

Janice says, "We like people who have strong family values. Our company is conservative that way. It must be hard for you as a professional to manage your home and your family. I'm sure you had to give up a lot. What made you decide to pursue a career instead of being a full-time mom?"

Wanda sighs. "That was a very personal decision. My husband and I balance our work and family. We do it together. I don't think I could be happy if I wasn't working with chemicals. I was the only girl in my third grade class with a chemistry set. My work entails a lot of creativity as well. That's what I thrive on."

"I suppose you have to be creative being a mom, too," Janice adds. "I have a son, and I'm constantly trying to figure out new ways to entice him to do his homework."

"I'm curious," Wanda says, "what was it about my résumé that seemed interesting to you when you called me for this interview?" (**She gently nudges the interviewer back to her professional background.**)

Janice glances down at the résumé in front of her. "One thing we all thought was interesting was the fact that your research topic dealt with fabric durability."

"Great. I'm fascinated with the molecular structure of different fabrics, particularly the synthetics. My research uncovered areas of study that have a unique relevance to this industry, particularly with regard to stain resistance. I worked with a team of eight researchers. We used state-of-the-art technology and probed the question from all angles. Last summer I delivered a paper in Montreal which was well received."

Janice says, "That's all very interesting. How was it working with a team of people?"

Wanda continues the interview talking about her experiences with her team and what she enjoyed about their contribution. She relaxes in the interview and feels more comfortable with the way it is progressing.

"Tell me about your experience in Montreal?" Janice asks.

"After I presented the paper, I met scientists from all over the world. These connections added new insights into my research and helped me consider angles I had not thought about."

"It must have been hard being that far away from your family," Janice says.

Wanda nods.

"How did you manage things while you were away?" Janice continues.

"By things, are you asking how I handled my absence from my family?"

"That's right. How did you manage all your household duties while you were away?"

"I am a bit confused about that question and how it relates to my work and my skill as a scientist. It frustrates me that most of this interview has been related to my family responsibilities instead of my responsibilities in the lab. I'm curious to know if I'm missing something. Tell me what it is you are concerned about so we can proceed talking about my work experience." (**Specifies the problem. Joins feelings with fact. Invites Janice to talk.**)

Janice responds, "I didn't mean to offend you. We recently hired someone we really liked, but she left the company after just two months. She was a mom who couldn't balance her home life and her work life."

"So, you're worried that any mom you interview will have the same problem, and you don't want to go through that again, right?" **(Shows compassion.)**

"I suppose I overdid it, didn't I? I wanted to get a sense of your commitment to work and personally I'm amazed by what you've accomplished with two kids. I can barely breathe with just one."

Wanda sits back. "I appreciate that recognition. Not everyone realizes the constant struggle. That in and of itself shows my commitment to work and my ability to persevere. I'm happy to talk about that. You are also welcome to talk to any of my professors who will vouch for my dedication to the team. It had troubled me, though, when I tried to talk about my work, we kept going back to my personal life. I understand your concerns now and your curiosity. Thank you for sharing that. How can we move forward from here?" **(Invites her to help resolve the problem.)**

"You've made it clear that you have a strong work ethic. That's important to us. Like I said this is a conservative company and even though family values are held high, so is a strong work ethic. How about we go forward with your telling me how you see your research skills specifically benefiting our division?"

ANALYSIS

Wanda struggled to get Janice to allow her to talk about her work experience. When she asked the question about what attracted Janice to her résumé she attempted to shift the spotlight away from personal issues. It worked for a while, but then Janice returned to asking personal questions. Wanda showed patience as well as compassion and curiosity. She finally, however, had to specify the problem as gently as she could.

Specify the Problem. Wanda knew that the personal questions Janice was asking were clearly illegal. Interviewers are not supposed to ask candidates, particularly women candidates, about their children or their child care plans. If Wanda had pointed out that the questions were illegal, she would have alienated Janice and lost the opportunity for continued interviews. She could have threatened a lawsuit unless Janice sent her to the next stage of interviews, but that would have been very risky. She elected to *say it just right* by specifying the problem gently, namely, that Janice kept asking questions that were unrelated to her work.

Invite the Other Person to Talk. Wanda invited Janice to talk in two places. First, when she specified the problem. She did this to give Janice a chance to explain what was going on. The second place was when she was looking for a resolution. She gave Janice a chance to reframe the interview and move forward.

Join Feeling with Fact. In two instances Wanda said she was "a bit confused." By using a nonexplosive feeling, like confusion, Wanda enabled Janice to help her understand what was happening in the interview. Wanda did this from an orientation of curiosity. She also showed compassion for Janice after the interviewer explained what happened with another employee as well as her own stress with finding balance in her life.

Resolve the Issue. By putting her feelings on the table and clearly specifying the problem within her limits, Wanda gave Janice a chance to resolve the problem. Wanda wanted to give Janice the power back and thereby put the interview back on track without creating bad feelings.

Conclusion

In this chapter we looked at two sticky interview situations. In the first we saw a situation most interviewers dread, namely, instances where the candidate clams up. It is very hard to conduct a strategic interview when the candidate does not talk. Paul gave Richard every opportunity to talk. He wanted Richard to leave the interview understanding why this job was not the best fit. Some interviewers do not care about the candidate's feelings. Once they decide to reject the candidate, they either end the interview quickly or ask abrupt, closed questions. Paul, who is probably a Sympathetic, preferred not to crush the candidate's spirit. He persisted and thereby turned a sticky, uncomfortable interview into a professional conversation that led Richard to the realization that the job was not for him—something Paul already knew.

The second case illustrated a sticky situation that many people who interview for jobs face. Wanda desired to get past the first round of interviews so she could showcase her scientific skills among fellow scientists. Even though Janice began the interview well by saying she wanted to get to know Wanda better, she crossed the line by probing personal areas that are legally sensitive. Wanda had to decide how much she was willing to endure. Once Janice went past that line,

Wanda gently but firmly explored ways to get the interview back on track. Many candidates would have suffered through the interview and allowed Janice to probe inappropriately, but Wanda had too much confidence in her work and herself as a scientist to allow that to happen. Wanda chose to *say it just right* even if she risked losing an opportunity to move forward in the interview process.

How do we handle the sticky etiquette situations that often come up in the modern workplace? The next chapter explores this question and shows us how Emily Post might *say it just right*.

Notes

1. Joan Curtis, *Strategic Interviewing: Skills and Tactics for Savvy Executives* (Westport, CT: Quorum Books, 2000).

2. Daniel Goleman, Richard Boyatzis, and Annie McKee, *Primal Leadership: Learning to Lead with Emotional Intelligence* (Boston: Harvard Business School Press, 2002), 44.

Chapter 10

Sticky Etiquette Situations

A book on sticky situations would be incomplete without looking at the awkward and uncomfortable situations that come up every day at work. These encounters are less extreme than the previous sticky situations we've observed, but they often put us in a dilemma. We wonder what is the appropriate thing to do. What would Emily Post tell us? In today's dynamic workplace with not only diversity between the sexes but also among nationalities and cultures the rules of the past may or may not apply.

As we examine these kinds of situations, we will sometimes apply the SIJR Model. Often, however, we need to only learn what behavior works and what behavior does not work by applying rules of etiquette.

Rate Your Etiquette Quotient[1]

To discover what you know about basic etiquette situations, take the following test to get your Etiquette Quotient. The higher your Etiquette Quotient, the easier it will be for you to handle sticky etiquette situations. Some questions come from the Professional Presence Quotient in Bixler and Dugan's work.

Answer True or False to each of the following statements.

1. A firm handshake is only offered to a businessman, not a businesswoman.
2. Socially, a man should wait for a woman in business to offer her hand before offering his.
3. It is okay to shake hands with someone while seated.
4. When two people are introduced, the woman is mentioned first.
5. During a business encounter, a man need not hold a chair for the female, stand up when she leaves the table, or open and close her car door.
6. The safest comfort zone for most people (distance-wise) is 3 to 6 feet.
7. Most people understand when you have call waiting and must take another call.
8. If you call someone and are disconnected because of something that happened on his or her end, you are responsible for redialing.
9. When using a speakerphone, it is not necessary to introduce everyone on the line.
10. Whether you are a man or a woman, if someone important walks into the room, you should stand up to shake hands.
11. It's polite to recap and welcome latecomers to meetings.
12. If you get invited to your boss's home and others in the office weren't, it's okay to mention your good fortune.

Learn your Etiquette Quotient in Appendix 1.

STICKY SITUATION # 20:
YOU'RE ON AN OVERNIGHT TRIP WITH A FLIRTY CO-WORKER

Belinda's boss just gave her and her co-worker, Brad, permission to go to an international meeting in Singapore. Belinda is thrilled about the trip because she has never flown that far nor been to Singapore. The company operates offices in Singapore that they will visit while there, but the majority of time will be consumed with the conference. When Belinda requested to go, she had no idea that Brad would ask to go as well. In fact, she did not learn of Brad's interest in the trip until her boss announced that they both would go. Belinda knew her face dropped when she heard that Brad was going. He and Belinda both work as marketing executives. Both have different accounts and rarely intermingle, but Brad's behavior has always caused Belinda to feel uncomfortable. He's one of those guys who seems to undress you with his eyes. He leers at her and has made suggestive, lewd remarks. The thought of traveling 18 hours in an airplane with him next to her gives her the creeps. Furthermore, once they arrive in Singapore, they are staying at the same hotel and renting a car together. The last day there, they travel across Singapore to visit the company offices before they return home.

Applying the Say It Just Right Model

Decision Points

Belinda weighs the costs. Belinda really wants to take this trip. It may be her only opportunity to go to Singapore. She's worked with the company for five years, and this is the first time her boss has agreed to send her overseas. She could request going next year, but there's no guarantee that Brad would not go again. Furthermore, if she declines this trip, her boss may not approve one for next year. He may consider her ungrateful. The conference they will attend is one of the biggest in her field. She will have an opportunity to learn new techniques, share ideas with others, and meet people from throughout the world. It's a huge chance for her. She decides that she must go.

Belinda sets the limits. Belinda is single, but Brad is married and has two small children. According to the office grapevine, he's never tried anything with anyone in the office. She suspects that he's all bark and no bite because he flirts but doesn't seem to take action. He's never made a direct pass at her. Nonetheless, she does not appreciate his lewd remarks. She will travel with Brad, but she will make it clear to him that if he does anything to cross the line, she will report his behavior to their boss and to Brad's wife.

Belinda determines the power sources. Brad has less tenure with the company than Belinda. He's relatively new and thereby more dispensable. He came to the company with impressive credentials, including a stint with Microsoft. He brings a lot of practical marketing knowledge that they all admired when he was hired. Belinda recognizes, however, that if she reports him for inappropriate behavior, it might cause a problem in the office. Before Belinda came, there were three marketing executives including their boss, all men. Belinda made every effort to fit in as one of the boys and not to make her femininity too obvious. If she reports Brad, her relationship with everyone will change.

PERSONALITY OVERLAY

Belinda recognizes Brad's Expressive personality. He craves being the center of attention. He's personable and easy to talk with. He often makes jokes. He draws others to him like a bee to honey. One of the reasons Brad excels in his work is that clients enjoy his personality. His Expressiveness enables him to win friends, but it also causes him to say things that he should not say. He does not think before he opens his mouth. She's noticed that she is not the only person Brad has offended with his indiscreet tongue.

Belinda, on the other hand, has some Expressive characteristics, but she is more of a Bold. She dislikes Brad's constant talk. She wonders how she'll stand being on the airplane with him if he decides to chat with her the entire 18 hours. She recognizes her own impatience, but she also knows that to make this trip tolerable for both of them, she'll have to adapt her style. She can't expect Brad to change.

SAY IT JUST RIGHT CONVERSATION

Belinda walks into Brad's cubicle and sits down. "We've got to talk."

He looks at her and grins. "I'm all ears. What do you want to talk to me about?"

"Before we go to Singapore, it would be good for us to set some ground rules."

He leans back and sighs. "This is going to be a glorious trip. I can't wait to get you all to myself."

She glares at him. "That's exactly what I'm talking about. I am not interested in playing games with you—"

"Whoa, an angry woman. I love it. You know your eyes get bluer when you're mad. How 'bout we duke it out?"

She takes a breath. "Brad, I'm not joking here. We're going to be together for many hours during this trip. It can be a great experience for us or it can be horrific. It's your choice."

"I've never had a woman tell me an experience with me was horrific. Trust me, it'll be great." He grins again.

"Is it not possible to have a serious conversation with you?"

He laughs.

"Look, Brad, I think I got off on the wrong foot here. Let me start over. I know you are as thrilled as I am to be going on this trip. It's a great opportunity for both of us. It could be a career launcher. I'm determined to make the most of it. I suspect you are, too. I'm curious to know what we can do to help each other do that." **(Invites Brad to talk.)**

"I've made a list of people I know who are going," he said, sitting up. "I'm planning to contact them and set up one-on-ones during the conference. Want me to include you?"

"No, I'd prefer to make informal contacts while there, but thanks. How about we agree to go our separate ways during the conference? You go have your meetings, and I'll float around with people I meet there. If we make some decent contacts, we can compare notes and introduce each other. What do you think?"

"Oh, I get it. You don't want to be seen with me."

She sighs. "It has nothing to do with that. We just have a different style of working the crowd. Tell me what would work for you. I suspect you don't want me hanging around while you meet with all these contacts, right?"

He nods. "Well, that might be a little strange. You're right. Let's plan to work it our own ways."

"There's one other thing, Brad. I don't like the way you openly flirt with me. If you do that in front of people at the conference, it will put us both in an awkward situation. I know you're just being—well, friendly—" **(Specifies the problem.)**

"You're just too much fun to tease. It's hard not to push your buttons."

"What can I do to help you 'not push my buttons'?" **(Invites Brad to talk.)**

He scratches his head. "Can't think of a thing."

"Brad, come on. Why do you tease me so much and not the others? It can't be just because I'm the only woman in the office. Tell me what is going on here." **(Continues to invite him to talk.)**

"I suppose it's just me. I had three sisters and that's how I dealt with them. They never minded my cutting up with them."

"How does your wife respond when you 'cut up' with other women?"

He chuckles. "She's used to it. She knows how I am. It's no big deal."

"I have to tell you, Brad, it is a big deal to me. I'm a pretty easy-going person, but I've been tempted to cite you for sexual harassment. Your comments about my clothes, about my hair, about my body, about how I smell are too suggestive. You've come very close to crossing the line." She pauses. "Although I now understand that you don't really mean it the way it comes across, someone else might not be as patient as I've been."

"You are a very attractive woman, and I just can't—"

"That's not relevant. It is not professional. I'm a marketing executive, just like you. When you say things like that to me, it puts me down, belittles me as a professional woman." **(Joins feelings with facts.)**

"I have a lot of respect for you and your work. I never meant to put you down."

"I know that now." She takes a breath. "We have a chance to build a strong working relationship on this trip. Let's give it a try. Are you willing?"

"Sure. What do you want me to do?"

"Better still. Why don't you tell me what you can do to curtail your need to 'cut up' with me?" **(Invites him to resolve the issue.)**

He takes a deep breath. "I'll not mention anything about the way you look. How's that?"

"Anything else?"

"Maybe we can limit our discussions only to work. And, I won't press you to eat or drink with me."

Belinda smiles. "All that sounds great. I suspect, though, we'll talk about things other than work, but if it feels uncomfortable to me, I'll let you know. Deal?"

They shake on it.

Analysis

Belinda started the discussion with Brad as a typical Bold. She got right to the point and wanted him to play her game. Brad, on the other hand, refused to join in. He toyed with her. Rather than get angry and impatient with him, she recognized what she'd done, and she started over. She specified the problem with an acknowledgment of the positive consequences for working as a team during this conference. He picked right up on that. She could have ended the discussion once she got his willingness to work together, but she recognized that she had not broached the real problem—his inappropriate behavior.

Had she begun by addressing his tendency to say unprofessional things to her, she might have lost him. His constant teasing protected him from talking seriously with her. She had to break that down before she could get to the real issue. With genuine curiosity, she wondered what she did that stirred him to tease her so hard. Once he opened up, she showed compassion but within her limits. She said she understood him better and recognized he was not saying those things to deliberately hurt her. Nonetheless, she told him his behavior was unacceptable. Her curiosity and compassion enabled her to draw him in to help resolve the problem. Knowing Brad and the fact that he behaves this way with all women, it is doubtful that this one conversation will change his behavior. For that reason Belinda suggested that she would immediately let him know when she felt he'd crossed the line.

Specify the Problem. She began in more general terms. She told him she didn't like the way he openly flirted with her. Later she clarified what troubled her: talking about her clothes, her hair, her body, and how she smells.

Invite the Other Person to Talk. Being a Bold, Belinda struggled to remain patient. When Brad evaded her invitations to talk, however, she pushed him. Finally, once he told her the way he "cut up" with his sisters, Belinda gained a better understanding of him.

Join Feeling with Fact. Again being a Bold, it was hard for Belinda to verbalize how the lewd comments made her feel. When she recognized that Brad wasn't getting it, she put her feelings into nonexplosive words. She told him she felt put down and small. Once Brad heard her and explained that was not his intent, the conversation took a turn.

Resolve the Issue. Belinda understood that it would be difficult for Brad to change his behavior. He treats all women the same way. Even his wife, according to Brad, had grown accustomed to his behavior. Nonetheless, Belinda created awareness, and she set limits letting him know how to behave around her, particularly at the conference.

STICKY SITUATION #21:
HOW TO EXTRICATE YOURSELF FROM A TALKER

Rita is a software engineer. She spends a lot of her time at her computer. Her work demands intensity. When she's in the middle of a project, it's difficult for her to break away. Her co-worker, Art, is a training specialist. He helps orient people to the new software designs that Rita's department develops. Likable, friendly Art has just one flaw. He does not recognize when he's overstayed his welcome. Rita knows Art does not mean to interrupt her. She suspects he gets bored or needs a break from his work. He spends much of the week on the road. While in the office, he becomes restless and perhaps hungry for companionship. He comes into Rita's office, sits down, and talks. He could stay 30 minutes to an hour. Rita does not wish to hurt his feelings, but his "visits" often come when she's either trying to meet a deadline or in the middle of a project that requires her full attention. She's tried to gracefully extricate herself, but Art doesn't get the message. Once when she told him she had an appointment and had to leave, he followed her out of the office, talking the entire time!

APPLYING THE SAY IT JUST RIGHT MODEL

DECISION POINTS

Rita weighs the costs. Art comes into her office about once a week and stays about 30 minutes. He travels the rest of the time. It annoys Rita, but Art's interruptions are not that frequent. If she talks to him about it, he may get offended. If she offends him, he will stop coming to visit her. Rita realizes that if Art stops visiting her, it really would not matter. She likes him; he's friendly and personable, but he's not a close friend. There are others in the office with whom he can talk and others she'd prefer to be with. Nonetheless, Rita does not wish to hurt Art's feelings.

Rita sets the limits. Rita realizes that she can work out a plan for Art to talk with her that fits in with her work schedule. She cannot always know when she'll be in the middle of a deadline, but if she creates a plan, she could gain control of these "unscheduled" visits. She decides that she will allow Art 30 minutes a week. Gaining a sense of when he'll come and for how long (it *will* have an end) releases her from permanently closing the door on him.

Rita explores the power sources. Art has been with the company for a long time. People like him, and he's good at his job. He holds no power over Rita, but if she wishes to move up in the company, having Art as a friend and advocate might assist her. She decides to handle the situation without confronting Art in an SIJR Conversation.

NEXT STEPS

Rita creates a plan for dealing with Art. She finds out from the office manager when Art will be in the office and when he's scheduled to travel. She posts his in-days on her calendar. When Art comes into her office, she shuts down her computer and spends the allotted time (30 minutes) fully engaged with him. He tells her many interesting stories about experiences on the road and with the company. After about 30 minutes, if Art does not rise to leave, Rita tells him she's got to get back to work. Usually this is enough for Art to go, now that she's spent "quality" time with him. When she has a deadline to meet on Art's in-days, she sends him an e-mail to let him know that she's working on a special project. She invites him to have a cup of coffee at a later time.

Once Rita gained more control on the visits and wasn't surprised by his intrusions, she began to look forward to Art's stories. They have since become close friends.

STICKY SITUATION #22:
WHOSE TURN IS IT TO PICK UP THE CHECK?

Adelaide and Ricky work as pharmacists in a large drug store. They have gone to lunch together three times. The first time, Adelaide agreed to pay because Ricky forgot to bring his credit card. He told her he'd make it up to her the next time. During their next lunch together, Ricky had to leave early to meet his wife for a parent-teacher meeting at school. He rushed out before the check was delivered and once again, Adelaide paid for both their lunches. During their third time out, another friend joined them. This time, Adelaide had to leave early. When she rose to leave, Ricky said, "Why don't you just leave me 10 bucks, and I'll bring you the change." Adelaide was surprised since she'd paid for lunch on the two previous occasions, but she didn't want to make a big deal of it in front of the other person. She handed

Ricky a 10-dollar bill. Ricky never gave her the change. She sus-pects that 10 dollars paid not only for her sandwich but for Ricky's as well.

APPLYING THE SAY IT JUST RIGHT MODEL

DECISION POINTS

Adelaide weighs the costs. Ricky and Adelaide earn the same income. She sees no reason for Ricky not to either pay for his own meal or to occasionally pay for Adelaide's. Because they work together every day, Adelaide doesn't want to cause a rift, but she feels as if Ricky is taking advantage of her. He has never thanked her for the lunches she's paid for, and he's never offered to pay her back. She's noticed that Ricky tends to cut corners in other ways at work as well. She won-ders about his integrity and decides that even if he gets angry with her and refuses to have lunch with her again, she'll feel better about herself if she confronts him.

Adelaide sets the limits. Clearly Ricky is trying to get as much out of Adelaide as he can. She doubts that he's forgotten that she's paid for his lunch now three times. She decides that she will no longer go to lunch with him unless he pays for his own meal. Even when their lunch break coincides, she prefers to eat alone.

Adelaide examines the power sources. Both Adelaide and Ricky came to the pharmacy at about the same time. Both have similar expe-rience and credentials. Adelaide has a great relationship with their boss. She's been told that she has the ability to become the head phar-macist if she continues working there. She suspects that Ricky, who often leaves early and comes to work late, has not had such glowing reviews. Even though Adelaide does not want to hurt the good work-ing relationship she has with Ricky, she sees that she holds a stronger power base than he does.

PERSONALITY OVERLAY

Adelaide is probably a Sympathetic. If she'd been a Bold, she would have demanded that Ricky pay for the second lunch. A Technical would have kept a clear record of what was owed her and presented it without conscience to Ricky. An Expressive would not have said anything to Ricky about the money owed but would also have looked for any alternative rather than to eat alone. Being a Sympathetic, Adelaide showed compassion for Ricky when he had to duck out early and when he forgot his credit card. It wasn't until he asked her for money on their third lunch outing, that she realized that Ricky was taking advantage of her good nature.

Ricky is probably neither a Technical nor a Sympathetic. He could be a Bold who recognizes that he can get something for nothing. He may also be an Expressive who cannot see Adelaide's discomfort. If he is more Expressive than Bold, he won't want to damage the relationship he has with Adelaide. A Bold personality is less concerned about the friendship than he is about being cornered or trapped in an awkward position.

Say It Just Right Conversation

Because Adelaide and Ricky do not have an opportunity to talk privately at work, she agrees to join him for lunch. Once they sit down, she says, "Ricky, I've been meaning to talk to you. I'm glad we could have lunch today."

"Sure thing." He picks up the menu. "I love this place. They have the best subs in town. Don't you think?"

Adelaide nods. "I prefer the salads. But, yeah, the subs aren't bad."

"What do you think about the new regs they're putting on us?"

"I'm okay with them. It'll just mean more paperwork. But, that's nothing new."

"You got that right. By the way, can you cover for me this afternoon? I've got a doctor's appointment and have to duck out about fifteen minutes early."

Adelaide sighs. "Ricky, I've covered for you every day this week. What's going on?"

He shrugs. "It's just hard to do everything. You know how it is."

"I sure do. I've got a three-year-old at home, remember?"

The waiter puts their lunch in front of them.

"Ricky, I hope you're not planning on my paying for your lunch again today?"

He looks up from his sandwich. "What do you mean?"

"I mean, we've been to lunch together three times, and I've paid for my lunch and yours each time. I'm curious to know when you might reciprocate." (**Specifies the problem.**)

"I hadn't realized that you paid for lunch every time. Didn't I pay last time?" The innocence in his voice almost makes Adelaide laugh.

"Come on, Ricky. I gave you 10 bucks to cover a four-dollar lunch. What I want to know is whether or not I'm going to be the one paying for lunch whenever we eat together?"

"I plan to pay for my lunch today," he says with a sniff.

"Look. I didn't mean to make you mad, but you know I can't afford to pay for both our lunches all the time. I like eating with you and talking about stuff at work. But, neither of us makes that kind of money. What do you think we should do about it?" **(Invites Ricky to talk.)**

He shifts around. "I said I'd pay for my lunch today and how 'bout I pay for yours, too. That suit you?"

"I value our friendship and want us to continue to have these lunches. I appreciate your willingness to pay for my lunch today. But, let's just start over from here. Why don't we each pay for our own lunches from now on." **(Joins feeling with fact.)**

"I don't want you to feel as if I owe you."

"Would paying for my lunch today make you feel better?" **(Looking for resolution.)**

"Yeah. And we'll go Dutch from then on. Sound good?"

Adelaide says, "That works for me."

ANALYSIS

Adelaide knew she could not change Ricky's behavior. When he asked for her to cover for him again, she recognized that he is the kind of person who will always ask or take a little more. It was up to her to set some limits. The beginning of their conversation enabled her to get a better feel for Ricky's personality type. The way he spoke casually about everything and his relaxed manner about the previous lunches all suggested he's an Expressive and not a Bold. Dealing with an Expressive, she used a positive consequence he'd relate to, namely, that she'd like to continue the lunches. She recognized that neither of them have the resources to pay for two lunches each time they eat out. Adelaide also dealt with Ricky's defensiveness by asking him for a solution that might work.

Specify the Problem. Adelaide did not specify the problem right away. When she told Ricky she wanted to talk to him, he didn't ask what she wanted to say. Instead he shifted the conversation to himself and thereby gave away his Expressive personality style.

Invite the Other Person to Talk. Adelaide invited Ricky to talk on several occasions. The first happened when she specified the problem and asked him when he'd reciprocate. Later she asked him what he suggested they do to resolve the problem. She elicited a defensive response from him when she asked, "What I want to know is if I'm going to be the one paying for lunch whenever we eat together?"

Her intent with this question was not to invite the other to talk, but to share her frustration.

Join Feeling with Fact. Adelaide told Ricky that she valued their friendship. She made it clear, however, that she could not continue to have lunch with him if she had to pay for both lunches. She showed appreciation for his willingness to pay for her lunch today, but she did not want him to do that as a martyr. Her willingness to begin with a clean slate opened the door for a resolution that Ricky could participate in.

Resolve the Issue. Because Ricky tends to take advantage of people, he will probably cross the line again. Adelaide must prepare herself for that eventuality. They agreed for him to pay for her lunch today but from now on they'd go Dutch. In the future if Ricky has a crisis (no wallet or no credit cards), Adelaide will likely have to confront him again.

As far as etiquette is concerned, when two colleagues eat lunch together, they split the bill. If you take your subordinate or a client to lunch, you pay.

Sticky Situation #23:
Traveling with Your Boss

Louisa works as an associate professor of history at a major university. Her dean, Dr. Marshall, invited her to attend a national conference in Texas to deliver a paper with him. Louisa is excited about the opportunity to go to this conference. She and Dr. Marshall have worked hard to prepare the material for the presentation. Recently, she learned that she and Dr. Marshall would travel to Texas together. They will stay in the same hotel and share taxis to get around the city. In all likelihood they will eat most of their meals together. Dr. Marshall knows other people at the conference, but Louisa knows no one except Dr. Marshall.

She worries that she will seem a burden to her dean. She thinks he will feel obligated to introduce her to anyone they meet and will not wish to leave her on her own. She also worries about how she will handle certain expenses. Who, for example, pays for the taxi or tips the driver? Who pays for the meals? Although the department pays for the major expenses, it does not cover drinks or other incidentals. Just because Dr. Marshall is a man and is the dean, is he required to pay for everything?

APPLYING THE SAY IT JUST RIGHT MODEL

DECISION POINTS

Louisa weighs the costs. Louisa wants to impress Dr. Marshall with her independence. She's been to conferences alone and met many new, interesting people. The last thing she wants is for Dr. Marshall to wish he'd never included her in this conference. If the presentation goes well, they might have opportunities to travel to other universities to talk about their research. She wants Dr. Marshall to see her as an asset and not a liability. If she talks to him ahead of time about how to handle miscellaneous expenses, he may consider her foolish or naïve. If she does not talk to him, they won't have a clear understanding, and that may produce some awkward moments.

Louisa sets limits. Louisa decides that she will talk to Dr. Marshall and tell him she does not expect him to include her when he's interacting with his colleagues. She will also tell him she'd like to set some parameters about expenses before they go in order to avoid misunderstandings.

Louisa examines the power sources. All the obvious power lies with Dr. Marshall. Louisa knows that if she does not assert herself with Dr. Marshall, she'll appear powerless. But if she does so beforehand, she can establish limits and enable both of them to have a much more productive trip.

PERSONALITY OVERLAY

We don't know a lot about Dr. Marshall's personality. Because he invited Louisa to join him and because he seems open to working with her, we might assume he is neither a Bold nor an Expressive personality. Bolds and Expressives are hard to pin down to work on a project. Expressives might invite others to join them at the conference, but they'd prefer to take center stage during the presentation, rather than allow the other person to present jointly as it sounds Dr. Marshall has done. He may, therefore, be a Sympathetic or a Technical. Lisa can observe Dr. Marshall's behaviors to determine which.

For example, if Louisa mentions her concerns to Dr. Marshall, and he tells her how it was done in the past with little opportunity for discussion, she knows he is probably a Technical. Most Technicals pay attention to the matters that worry Louisa. They want to make certain that each person pays his or her own way, and no one gets a "free" ride. If, on the other hand, Dr. Marshall responds with genuine interest about her concern about these matters, he is probably a Sympathetic. In that case Louisa will have to push him a little harder to clarify the parameters.

Say It Just Right Conversation

Louisa enters Dr. Marshall's office. "I'd like to talk to you about the upcoming trip to Houston."

He motions for her to sit down. "What is it?"

"I know that you've been to this conference many times, and you know a lot of people there. I'm flattered that you invited me to participate with you this year—"

"I highly respect your work. Your perspective on the material will be an asset and will bring a fresh new approach."

"Thank you for that. I thought it would be a good idea to clarify a few things before we go." (**Specifies the issue.**)

"Sure." He leans forward.

"Because this is my first trip to this national conference, I want to have a chance to meet people from universities all over the country. I don't want you to feel as if you have to drag me along with you all the time. Why don't we agree to go our separate ways after the presentation? I'm sure there are sessions I want to go to that you have no interest in."

"Absolutely," he said. "I just assumed that we'd do that."

"Good. Also, I wondered about how the expenses worked. I know the university will pay for our meals and everything, but what about miscellaneous expenses?" (**Asks for clarification.**)

"Yes, we'll put in a request after we get back. You'll want to keep all your meal receipts. The meal allowances usually do not cover everything."

"How will we work it when we eat together? Will we each have a separate receipt?" (**Searches for clarification by inviting Dr. Marshall to talk.**)

"Oh, no. We can work that out between us. Usually I put it on my credit card, and the colleague pays me back what's owed in cash. Last year, Paul accompanied me. He seemed fine with that arrangement." (**Offers a resolution.**)

"If I want a glass of wine with dinner, then, I can just pay you in cash afterwards?"

"Sure, unless we agree for me to treat you to a glass of wine. I'd like to be able to do that, on occasion," he adds.

"I have no problem with that so long as we're clear. It can get confusing nowadays, and I don't want either of us to get frustrated. Some guys feel as if they must pay for everything. And, that's just not fair." **(Joins feeling with fact.)**

He says, "I do have a tendency to be a bit old fashioned. But, I've learned that most of you modern women want to pay your own way. That's fine with me. I'm glad we had this discussion so we both know what to do before we depart next week. Thank you for initiating it."

"I also appreciate your candor. I'm really excited about this trip, and I want everything to go well. Just to clarify, then, I'll plan to go my own way after the presentation. If we share meals together, I'll pay you for whatever exceeds our meal allowances. Does that sound right?" **(Summarizes the resolution.)**

"Good deal."

ANALYSIS

It doesn't take long for Louisa to realize that Dr. Marshall is a Sympathetic. Once she told him she wanted permission to go her own way, and he responded, "I just assumed . . ." she knew she was likely not dealing with a Technical. Technicals leave little to chance.

Rather than specify a *problem* as is often the case in sticky situations, Louisa specifies an issue. She is looking for clarity. To do that, she must use the same skills, but she applies them in a different manner.

Specify the Problem. Louisa first specified the issue of clarification, and then she continued to push until she felt the issue had clarity.

Invite the Other Person to Talk. This situation was nonconfrontational and one that required a joint solution. Louisa invited Dr. Marshall to share what had been done in the past and to clarify for her what he expected of her. He made it clear they would "work things out together." When he suggested he might buy her a glass of wine, it showed her that the procedures were not so cut and dried.

Join Feelings with Fact. Louisa explained that she wanted to avoid negative feelings and that was why she initiated the conversation. His appreciative response told her she made the right decision.

Resolve the Issue. When the issue is clarification, it helps to summarize what has been resolved at the end as we saw Louisa do.

CONCLUSION

In this chapter we looked at four sticky etiquette situations. The Decision Points phase of the SIJR Model is always important because it is there that we opt to either proceed or not to proceed with the SIJR Conversation. With sticky etiquette situations, particularly, you may choose not to approach the other person. In the first situation, Belinda had little choice. If she were to make this trip with Brad, she had to confront him. Belinda faced a larger question than what was proper decorum on a trip with a colleague. She faced the question of whether or not Brad had crossed the sexual harassment line. When Belinda realized that Brad meant no harm with his remarks, she relaxed and told him what was appropriate and what was not. Again, Brad may not change his behavior, but Belinda made it clear she would report him if he misbehaved.

As for Rita and Art, Rita recognized that she could manage the situation without confronting Art. During the Decision Point analysis, she realized that a confrontation might seriously jeopardize their working relationship. A few minor changes in the way she dealt with Art enabled her to avoid having to say anything to him.

In the situation with the slippery co-worker, Adelaide had to confront Ricky to maintain her own self-worth. She could not allow Ricky to continue taking advantage of her.

Finally, Louisa could have either talked with Dr. Marshall or dealt with her concerns without talking to him. She made the choice to talk to him in order to get clarification, but in her Decision Point analysis she could have just as easily decided to avoid talking to him and discovered the appropriate procedures in another manner.

The next chapter explores how to apply the Say It Just Right Model in the virtual world. Today, we spend much of our workday in virtual conversations with people at their computers. How do we deal with a sticky situation when the person we are confronting lives on another continent?

NOTE

1. Susan Bixler and Lisa Scherrer Dugan, *5 Steps to Professional Presence: How to Project Confidence, Competence, and Credibility at Work* (Avon, MA: Adams Media Corporations, 2001), xxi–xvi.

Chapter 11

Sticky E-situations

If you are anything like me, you are spending more and more hours in the workday at your computer. Perhaps, you are out and about but sending and receiving messages via your handheld device. Communication in today's work world goes beyond the face-to-face interactions or even the telephone contacts of the past. We zip off more and more e-mails and texts than ever before. David Shipley and Will Schwalbe in their book *Send* tell us that the Bush administration was expected to turn over 100 million e-mails to the National Archives in contrast to 33 million from the Clinton administration in 2001.[1] Most of us don't need statistics to tell us how much we depend on e-mail to conduct our daily businesses. In fact, a large telecommunications company initiated a weekly "no e-mail" day similar to the "casual" Fridays. At first the staff balked, but after the first day, they enjoyed not having to deal with e-mail. In a poignant example, one staff member contacted another by telephone. During their conversation they realized that they worked in the same facility and after a bit longer time, they realized that they sat a few cubicles away from one another. These realizations demonstrate for us that we have become overly reliant on e-mail and other electronic communication.

Before we step back and examine the sticky situations that evolve from the e-mail explosion, we must look at when it is appropriate to e-mail and when another form of communication serves us better. In addition to examining e-mail in this fashion, we must also consider instant messages (IM's), text messaging, and all other forms of e-communication.

One of the biggest problems with e-communication is the "send" button. As soon as you hit that button, you cannot turn back. Furthermore, e-communication prevents us from judging a reaction to our message. In Chapter 1 we looked at the power of nonverbal communication. Via countless nonverbal messages, we pass along our feelings and the underlying "intent" of the communication. When we say to a colleague, "That report really should go to the boss," do we mean it *should*, meaning the boss needs to get it, but don't send it for goodness sakes! Or, do we mean, he *should* get the report, and yes send it, like, now! Are we joking? Are we being sarcastic? Are we deeply affected? We cannot convey any of these feelings through e-communication where the risk of misunderstanding skyrockets. Yet, more and more of us are writing notes to colleagues, clients, subordinates, and bosses and expecting those one-way communication notes to convey meaning.

How can we take advantage of the amazing convenience of e-communication and avoid the risks of miscommunication?

CHOOSING THE RIGHT KIND OF COMMUNICATION

When we look at communication of all types, we must evaluate the medium in which we communicate. In the past we had fewer choices, namely face to face, telephone, or written letter. For years people wondered about the best time to use each of these media. Clearly, when we had something urgent to convey or when we wanted to make our message particularly personal, we chose a face-to-face interaction. When the message was less personal, we moved down the continuum to telephone communication and finally to the least personal, the business letter. After years of struggle, that is, when we sent letters when we should have called or when we called when we should have communicated in person, we finally figured it out.

Today, however, we have many more choices and those sheer numbers add to the confusion around what to do and when. For example, a letter no longer seems impersonal. In fact, because we get so few letters or handwritten notes, we take notice when one comes across our desk. We appreciate the time it takes to actually put a letter in an envelope and attach a stamp. These efforts suggest something much more meaningful than they did in the past. The telephone call, which used to be more impersonal, has become an "interaction." Indeed, we've reached a new crossroads in communication where we must decide on a medium for our message not based on convenience alone but based on purpose and intent.

WHEN TO USE E-COMMUNICATION?

E-mail

- When communicating with a large group of people.

- When communicating simple, direct, clear facts, for example, "We're meeting at the corner of Fifth Street at noon."

- When only one or two responses will give you an answer. Not when trying to reach a complex decision.

- When communicating across continents or great distances. (Although telephone services, such as Skype, have become so inexpensive that phone contacts, too, can be an alternative to e-mail if distance is the only obstacle).

- When setting up a telephone appointment or a face-to-face appointment.

- When including a link to an article or blog you think someone might enjoy reading.

- When you do not want to interrupt the other person. For example when the other person is in a meeting, on an airplane, attending a wedding or funeral, or otherwise unavailable by telephone.

Texting and IM's

- Texting is a great alternative to cell phone conversations in public. Who wants to listen to you set up your big presentation or buy your car?

- When you need an *instant* response. But, how often do you *really* need an instant response? Some examples of when an instant response might be necessary include when you are lost and need to get to an important meeting; your flight was cancelled and you need to contact others before they depart their cities; documents were not received; or you need to locate your teenage daughter.

- When you know the other person is unavailable by e-mail or cell phone and it's the best way to send a *short* message.

- When there is too much noise around for you to talk on the phone and you want to send someone a short message.

Most of us use e-communication much more extensively than necessary. We do this out of convenience. We do not wish to pick up the telephone because we either get voice mail or we get the person and must thereby interact. Talking takes longer than e-mailing. Furthermore, telephone tag used to be a huge annoyance and a stumbling block to doing business. The cell phone has nearly eliminated telephone tag.

Cell phones, however, bring their own sets of problems. Are we disturbing an important meeting? Is it intrusive to call people on their cells when we do not know them very well? Most bosses do not think twice about calling their subordinates on their cell phones and they expect them to be available 24/7. But, is that fair? People have lives outside of work. The cell phone has literally brought our work lives into every facet of our existence, whether having a romantic dinner with our spouse or attending our child's soccer game.

Shipley and Schwalbe describe six essential types of e-mail communication, namely, requesting, responding, informing, thanking, apologizing, and connecting.[2] Notice that the authors do not include anything remotely related to dialogue. In other words, when we really need to talk to someone—have a conversation about something, brainstorm ideas, or hear alternatives—e-mail is not the best choice. There's no question, then, that e-mail is not the way to conduct an SIJR Conversation.

As we wrestle with the appropriateness of which form of communication to employ when, we find ourselves facing more and more confusing, sticky e-situations.

STICKY SITUATION #24:
A BOSS WHO E-MAILS SUBORDINATES WITH PERFORMANCE REVIEWS

Zack works in an international media development company. His boss, Tommy, is one of the vice presidents. Zack likes working for Tommy because Tommy leaves him alone to do his job. Each day Tommy sends him about 20 e-mails even though they work a few corridors away from one another in the same building.

Tommy's e-mails go to Zack and others on the team to inform them about various issues related to their projects or to request updates. Sometimes Tommy copies Zack on things he thinks Zack needs to know.

Zack's problem lies in his inability to talk to Tommy face to face. Whenever he asks (by e-mail, of course) for a face-to-face meeting, Tommy wants to know what the meeting is about. Once Zack tells him, Tommy responds with directives in order not to conduct the meeting. What surprised Zack, however, was when he received his annual performance review by e-mail:

To: Zack
From: Tommy
Subject: Annual Review
Your work is adequate. Please find attached my review. E-mail your responses or initial it and return to me.

Zack reviewed the comments, and he saw that Tommy had rated his work as adequate or very good but never outstanding. Zack felt dejected and wondered what he needed to do to improve his performance.

Applying the Say It Just Right Model

Decision Points

Zack weighs the costs. Zack realizes that if he does not learn how he can improve his performance, he will never achieve his goal to move up in this company. He knows that he will have to push Tommy hard to have a face-to-face interaction, and he realizes that Tommy will probably respond negatively if he criticizes him for sending the performance review by e-mail. Such actions might destroy the easy relationship they currently have. Zack decides that doing nothing will prolong the problem, and he will likely find himself in this same position next year when it will be tougher to nail Tommy down.

Zack sets limits. Zack decides that he will talk to Tommy about needing more face time. How can he perform his job if he never sees his boss and his boss never tells him what he expects? He decides to push for face-to-face interactions on all performance-related issues.

Zack determines the power sources. Tommy is the boss. If he wants to conduct performance reviews by e-mail, that's his choice. Zack suspects, however, that Tommy wants his staff to perform in an outstanding manner. The vice presidents in this company tend to compete with one another for higher recognition. If Tommy continues to use e-mail for performance evaluations, he will never achieve the kind of recognition Zack knows Tommy wants. Zack recognizes Tommy's competitive nature; he loves to be the first in the company to resolve issues, and he likes it when his team gets company perks. Knowing this about Tommy gives Zack a bit of leverage.

PERSONALITY OVERLAY

We do not know very much about Tommy except he is competitive and he does not like face-to-face interactions. These two clues suggest a Bold personality. We further suspect Tommy's Boldness because the efficiency and speed of e-mail attracts the Bold personality. Tommy is probably not a Sympathetic nor an Expressive because both of these styles enjoy meeting in person. In most instances people who overly embrace e-mail are Bolds.

SAY IT JUST RIGHT CONVERSATION

To: Tommy
From: Zack
Subject: Meeting
Dear Tommy,
I'd like to talk to you on Thursday at 2 P.M. about my recent performance review.
Thanks,
Zack

To: Zack
From: Tommy
Subject: Meeting
What is it you want to know?

To: Tommy
From: Zack
Subject: Meeting
Dear Tommy,
It would be better if we talked. I'll come to your office. Let me know if 2 P.M. does not suit.
Thanks,
Zack

To: Zack
From: Tommy
Subject: Meeting
Can't we handle this by e-mail? It's faster, and I've got a lot on my plate right now.

To: Tommy
From: Zack
Subject: Meeting
Dear Tommy,
I'll see you on Thursday at 2 P.M. It won't take longer than 30 minutes.
Thanks, Zack

Zack did not get another e-mail from Tommy related to their Thursday meeting. This time Zack chose not to go into detail about what he wanted to discuss. His persistence led to Tommy's agreement to a meeting, which in and of itself was a victory for Zack.

On Thursday at 2 P.M. Zack finds Tommy at his desk, sending e-mails. He knocks on the door frame.

Tommy looks up. "What is it you wanted that required a meeting?"

Zack sits across from him. "I'm concerned that my performance ratings are lower than I had hoped. I wanted to find out directly from you what your expectations are so I can aim for them and improve myself."

Tommy pushes back from the desk. "I could've told you that by e-mail. You just need to get more accounts. You got three new ones this year and that's not exactly outstanding."

"I was reestablishing old accounts and managed to keep all of them, even some we've let slide for years. When I came on board this year, my main goal was to keep existing accounts. I've done that and added three new ones. That seems to me beyond an 'adequate' rating."

Tommy begins scanning through his e-mails. "When did I send you that e-mail about keeping existing accounts? I don't remember that."

"That was what you said to me on my first day of work. We actually had a conversation."

"No wonder," Tommy mutters. "I need a record of everything. Otherwise I can't keep up with what's going on."

"Tommy, I know how much you value e-mail communication. I also value its efficiency. There are some times, however, when e-mail can get confusing or even inefficient. I have to tell you I was surprised when I got the performance review by e-mail. It made me feel as if you didn't have the guts to face me." **(Specifies the problem, joins feeling with fact.)**

Tommy shrugs. "I suspected you wouldn't be happy with it. But, don't worry, I sent everyone's PR by e-mail. I always do."

"Performance reviews are a great way to keep people motivated. It helps them see ways they can grow. When you send them by e-mail, it's very impersonal, and for me it was de-motivating. How can you get the efficiency and high achievement you desire without de-motivating people?" **(Invites Tommy to talk.)**

"You're not suggesting I talk with everyone face to face? That would take days."

"I'm asking you what might be possible. Surely something exists between lengthy interactions with everyone and e-mail communication."

Tommy sighs and thinks. "Maybe I could send the performance review and ask if the person wants to meet." **(Looking for resolution.)**

"That would be better. Imagine, though, if you were me. You get this review that rates you adequate. You think you've done better than adequate. Your boss says in his e-mail, let me know if you want to meet. You're still feeling pretty lousy, aren't you?" **(Pushes him toward resolution.)**

"So, what do you think would work better?" Tommy asks.

"Maybe what we need is something more frequent than an annual review. That way both you and I could monitor the goals." **(Resolving the issue.)**

"I envision a lot of meetings," Tommy says with a sigh.

"Not necessarily. You could meet for 15 minutes with each person to set goals. Then, we could send you e-mails on the status of our goals every three months. If something goes astray, we could schedule a special meeting. How do you think that might work?"

"I could see that working. Fifteen-minute discussions to establish goals. Maybe each person could e-mail me their proposed goals ahead of the meeting to save time."

"I like that. So, when might we start this process?"

"You and I can start right now with our 15-minute discussion. Then, this afternoon I'll send out an e-mail announcing the new process and setting up the appointments for others on the staff."

ANALYSIS

Zack faced quite a challenge getting Tommy to agree to see him. Once he accomplished that goal, he had to help Tommy see how his performance review by e-mail affected him. Tommy is clearly a Bold. Zack showed patience and did not get defensive with Tommy's brusque communication style. When Tommy said, "I could've told you that by e-mail," Zack kept quiet. Zack did not get angry when Tommy began scrolling through his e-mails looking for documentation of what Zack remembered. Instead, he pushed forward and specified the problem even though he let his feelings show when he said, "We actually had a conversation." That sarcastic comment demonstrated Zack's humanness and his frustration.

Zack knows that Tommy will continue to abuse e-mail. He understands that e-mail is part of Tommy's management style. Zack set a small goal: To help Tommy recognize how performance reviews can be a useful tool to motivate. He played on Tommy's desire for efficiency and high achievement.

Specify the Problem. Zack did not jump right in with the main problem. Instead he waited for Tommy to warm up to the conversation. When he specified the problem (overuse of e-mail, particularly with performance reviews) he also joined feelings with fact.

Invite the Other Person to Talk. Being a Bold, Tommy did not offer much conversation. He often responded in quick, short sentences. Even though his style was abrupt and seemed to cut off conversation, Zack pushed forward. He realized he got Tommy's buy-in when he asked, "So what do you think would work better?"

Join Feeling with Fact. Zack could have told Tommy he was offended or hurt when his performance review arrived in his in-box. Instead he said he was surprised. Surprise is a less emotional word and would therefore not trigger as defensive a response. Later he used the term, de-motivating. He knew that Tommy wanted to keep the staff motivated in order to maintain performance at peak levels.

Resolve the Issue. Tommy could not envision anything but e-mail communication or long-winded face-to-face interactions. Zack pushed him to think harder and finally offered suggestions to help Tommy see the value of a combination of the two. Fifteen-minute interviews, prefaced with e-mail communication, and followed by e-mail monitoring seemed palatable and even preferable to Tommy.

Sticky Situation #25:
Proselytizing on the Company Blog

A large automotive company began an internal blog two years earlier. The CEO regularly posts messages to employees, and the HR division maintains the blog and keeps it active. Once employees became comfortable with blogging, they began to write comments and post new ideas. Recently one employee, Nichole, posted a blog about her experience after the birth of her child who was born with a severe medical disorder. She thanked the employees who prayed for her child's recovery and who helped her deal with the stress. Her blog entrees kept others informed about what the doctor said and how her son had fared during several operations. Everything seemed okay until her more recent comments. She wrote long entrees about how blessed she was to have her son alive and how the Lord watches out for people who love him. She quoted the Bible in several places. In a later comment she wrote several paragraphs about how her faith had gotten her through this trying time and what that meant to her. She encouraged people to pray everyday and to rejoice in the name of Jesus Christ.

Mickey heads the HR division. He's watched as Nichole's posts have become increasingly religious in nature. When the company developed the blog, they created stipulations that prevented people from using profanity or from writing prejudicial comments. Nichole's comments are not prejudicial per se, but her strong Christian views leave out the Jews, Muslims, and persons of other faiths or those of no faith who populate the large company. Mickey worries that some people might find Nichole's posts offensive.

Applying the Say It Just Right Model

Decision Points

Mickey weighs the costs. It took Mickey and his staff years to win approval from the CEO to initiate a blog. Mickey finally convinced the top executives that blogs enable people to share ideas, comment on policies, and connect with each other. It also provides a platform for the CEO to share his vision for the company in a personal manner. At the outset, Mickey struggled to convince people that the blog was a safe place for them to air their ideas or complaints. It also took awhile for the CEO to adjust to daily posting. Today, the CEO enjoys sharing his thoughts and responding to people throughout the company.

He often tells Mickey how much he likes the blog. When the CEO was traveling across the country recently, a woman came up to him, introduced herself, and said she worked in marketing for the company. Because of the blog, she felt comfortable enough to speak directly to the CEO. They had a great conversation, sharing similar interests as if they were two colleagues. Upon his return the CEO said to Mickey, "This has been the best communication tool we've ever had both internally and externally." Mickey realizes that if he muzzles Nichole, he will threaten the openness of the blog. But he also realizes that if he allows her to continue to proselytize, he puts the future of the blog in jeopardy.

Mickey sets limits. When the company began the internal blog, they decided not to monitor comments. They believed that if someone had the courage to write something, what they wrote should be posted for everyone to see, so long as the item contained neither profanity nor prejudicial statements. Mickey does manage the comments coming into the external blog, which is open to everyone in cyberspace. As for the internal blog, however, Mickey wants to maintain the sense of openness of a non-monitored blog. Nonetheless he must intervene with Nichole. He finds her comments increasingly prejudicial. Even though she does not say anything negative about people of other faiths or of no faiths, her intent is clear. He decides he can justify blocking her password if she continues to proselytize.

Mickey determines the power sources. The CEO is enthusiastic with the blog and how it has humanized him to the staff. He has sung Mickey's praises throughout the company. If Mickey suggests that he monitor the blog and screen its comments, the CEO will likely agree, but with reluctance. Mickey, however, prefers to deal directly with Nichole. She has strong personal ties with many people in the company. When her child was ill, everyone talked about it and rallied around her. If Mickey censors Nichole, she might complain to others and that could jeopardize the blog activity. Even though Mickey has a strong power base all the way to the CEO, Nichole also holds onto a strong base within the ranks. Given these considerations, Mickey decides to confront Nichole as gently as possible but within the limits he has set for himself, namely, no proselytizing.

PERSONALITY OVERLAY

Mickey imagines that Nichole is an Expressive. She enjoys being with people, and she's a talker. She has embraced the blog because she can share her feelings with so many people at once. Although her child's illness was a tragedy, she used his sickness to her advantage. She gained a lot of support and told anyone willing to listen about the latest condition of her son. Fortunately, her son recovered, but she continues to rehash what life might have been like had they not had God's help.

As an Expressive, she wants to remain on center stage. The recent blog posts appear to have taken the tone of wishing to save her friends who supported her through the ordeal. Saving them means they must embrace Jesus Christ as the Son of God.

Say It Just Right Conversation

Mickey sends Nichole an e-mail asking her to come see him. They agree to meet that morning at 10 o'clock.

"Good morning, Nichole, thanks for coming."

She sits down across from him. "No problem. I'm glad to have this opportunity to talk. We never see each other in the cafeteria like we used to."

"My lunch hour seems to have disappeared," Mickey says with a shrug. "How's Jamey?"

"Every day he's better. We are so blessed, not just with God's healing hand but also with the healing support the Lord sent to us through this company."

"I know your family is relieved to have all this behind you. What I wanted to talk to you about was the nature of your comments on the blog—"

"So many people were concerned about Jamey. They asked me how things were every second of the day. And, I cherished all their prayers and support. The blog was a great way to keep everyone up on what was happening. I appreciated that opportunity. Thank you so much for making the blog accessible to all of us. Even Mr. Harris asked me about Jamey when I saw him in the facility two months ago. That was amazing since I didn't think he even knew who I was."

"Mr. Harris is quite pleased with the blog and how it's connected everyone in the company. I'm not surprised he's reading your blog posts. But, what worries me is not that you shared updates on Jamey's condition. What worries me is that your posts are getting more and more religious in nature." **(Specifies the problem.)**

She smiles. "I'm so happy about what the Lord has done for me and my family. I want everyone I know to share in the joy. I'm ecstatic in

God's love through his Son, Jesus. I love the people here as if they were part of my own family, and—"

"It would seem to me, then, Nichole, that you would not want to offend anyone in the company, right?"

Her eyes widen. "Of course not. How could sharing the love of Jesus offend people?"

Mickey sighs. "That's the problem. We are a very large company with layers of people from different cultures and walks of life. Not everyone considers themselves Christian—"

"Then, I need to help them see the Light."

"No, Nichole, that is not your role. When you say that you need to help people see the light, it feels as if their way is wrong. Doing that is prejudicial because it shows a bias against other people's religions. I'm curious to know what you thought you were doing when you quoted verses of the Bible that suggested certain lifestyles were inappropriate." **(Invites Nichole to talk.)**

"The Bible is clear about homosexuality."

Mickey sits back. "In your view the Bible's clear. In other views, it's not so clear. The New Testament calls us to love one another regardless. Some might say that means love everyone, even gay people. But, I'm not here to argue points of the Bible. I simply want to bring to your attention how some of your blogging might offend people." **(Respecifies the problem.)**

"I know what the Bible says. I wanted to share the message with all the wonderful people here who helped me get through Jamey's illness. That's all."

"If I understand, then, your goal was to share your religious views because people helped you get through Jamey's illness. I'm sure that meant a lot to you. How can you remain open without offending others?" **(Invites Nichole to talk about resolution.)**

She shrugs. "Are you going to censor my blogs?"

Mickey says, "I'm frustrated because I don't want to censor anyone. The intent of the company blog was to create a sense of open communication. We've been quite successful with that. People in other parts of the country feel closer to headquarters and vice versa. It's been a great success. The external blog has helped us keep a good pulse on our customers. If we allow people to vent on controversial or prejudicial topics, which might offend others, we might turn people off; they'll quit reading the blog and quit posting. I want openness, but I also want discretion. I'm frustrated about how to do that. Can you help me here?" (**Joins feelings with facts.**)

"I suppose I took some liberties. I just felt so close to everyone, and I wanted to share my joy. Mickey, you just can't imagine the Light unless you've seen it. I want to share it with you. You can see it, too, if you—"

"How can you share that special joy without stepping on people's religious beliefs?" (**Asks for resolution.**)

Nichole thinks. "The Lord asked me to share the Good Word as part of his healing of Jamey. I see that as an important part of my mission—God's mission. It's what Jesus asked his disciples to do. I have to do what God asks me to do. If I post on the blog, I have to share the Lord's message. It's the way of God."

"I'm really sorry, Nichole, but you leave me with just one choice as I see it," Mickey says. "I have to ask you not to post on the blog and not to comment on other people's posts, unless you can keep your comments strictly professional. By professional, I mean, you can share your successes on the job or your work-related concerns, as others in the company do. If your comments cross the line and become prejudicial, I will have to remove your password access. I'm curious to know if you can think of any other alternatives." (**Resolving the issue.**)

Nichole frowns. "I'd like to have a chance to pray about this. Can I give you an answer tomorrow?"

Mickey rises. "That's fine. Meantime, I'm asking you not to put anything on the blog that has a religious tone. Will you agree to that?"

Nichole nods and rises. "Yes."

ANALYSIS

Mickey did not expect to change Nichole's beliefs. He was not even sure he could change her behavior as far as the blog was concerned. He wanted to raise her awareness about how her words might affect other people. Doing so did not seem to affect Nichole. She was determined that it was her duty to share her beliefs.

Being an Expressive, Nichole revealed her feelings but did not listen to Mickey. He had to interrupt her several times to make his point, and he had to respecify the problem. Mickey could have caught Nichole's attention had he stated his feelings more strongly. For example, he could have said the posts offended him and explained why.

Although Mickey asked Nichole to help him reach a suitable resolution, he stated clear limits. He wanted openness on the blog but nothing that might be prejudicial. Once Mickey knew that Nichole heard him, he shared his own frustration.

In the end Nichole wanted time to pray about this problem and was thereby reluctant to agree to the resolution. Mickey, however, pushed her to agree to stop putting her religious views on the blog. The final decision lies with Nichole. Is having blog access more important to her than spreading the Word? Whatever she decides, Mickey has accomplished his goal to stop her from proselytizing on the company blog.

Specify the Problem. The first time Mickey specified the problem, he used neutral words. He referred to her posts as "religious in nature." He chose not to use the more explosive term, proselytizing. He knew she'd get defensive and he wanted to minimize her defensiveness as much as possible. The second time he specified the problem, he did so around the feelings of others. He said he wanted her to know that her blogging might "offend" others. He showed compassion as he listened to her side of the story and as he urged her to help him find a solution.

Invite the Other Person to Talk. Mickey invited Nichole to talk on several occasions. Dealing with an Expressive, he had no trouble getting her to talk. The problem was getting her to talk about the *right* thing. She spoke openly about her beliefs but gave him nothing that might lead to resolution. Her inability to see any resolution beyond her own determination suggested to Mickey that he'd have to resolve the issue in his own way. He approached her with curiosity, almost begging her for suggestions. But, she remained firm in her position that she was doing what God asked her to do.

Join Feeling with Fact. It was not until the end of the conversation that Mickey shared his feeling of frustration. He let Nichole know that he wanted the blog to be an open forum. He wanted her to continue to post but only about her work successes and concerns. He did not want her to turn the blog into a place where people espoused their religious views. In sharing his frustration, he hoped to gain her support and willingness to change.

Resolve the Issue. In the end, Mickey resolved the issue and then asked for Nichole's agreement. He advised her that if she did not agree to the blogging rules, he would remove her password access. This resolution was heavier than Mickey would have liked, but he could see no alternative without Nichole's help and willingness.

Conclusion

In this chapter we looked at sticky e-situations and how to apply the Say It Just Right Communication Model to resolve those situations. Both cases required a face-to-face conversation. Zack struggled to get Tommy to agree to a meeting, but once he did, he managed to express his needs within the limits he set for himself. Zack ran the risk of Tommy never agreeing to meet in the first place. Had that happened, Zack might have decided to leave the company. As it turned out, Zack helped Tommy see the importance of face-to-face contact with staff. Although he only got 15-minute interviews, he considered that a step up from zero face time.

In the second situation we saw a company that had the courage to initiate an open internal blog. After years of working with the top executives, Mickey finally got the blog approved. Mickey did not wish to see it destroyed because one employee started using that platform for her own purposes. If Mickey had allowed Nichole to continue to proselytize, he faced the possibility of others sharing their religious or political views and the blog becoming a tool for extremists. Undoubtedly the CEO would then shut down the entire system.

Nichole's determination to share her views may be stronger than Mickey's desire to keep the blog open. He may have to block her password. He realized that doing so might inflame Nichole to share her passionate views in other ways. If that should happen, Mickey will need to have another conversation with Nichole and take whatever action may be necessary.

Be aware that *saying it just right* does not always stop the behavior. It does, however, help people understand the issue in a way that invites them to participate in the resolution.

Notes

1. David Shipley and Will Schwalbe, *Send: The How, Why, When & When Not of Email* (New York: Canongate, 2007), 6.
2. Ibid., 35.

Chapter 12

Sticky Situations on the Home Front

Throughout this book we looked at various sticky situations that arise in the workplace and how to talk our way out of those situations by using the Say It Just Right Model of communication. The first step in the SIJR Model was to examine the three Decision Points:

- Weigh the costs for acting or for not acting.

- Set your limits. If you have a conversation, what are you willing to do? What are you not willing to do?

- Determine the power sources. Where does the power lie? Are you feeling powerless in this situation?

After we examined the Decision Points and before we initiated the conversation, we looked at the Personality Overlay. We did this using James Brewer's BEST personality styles. I chose Brewer's model because it is easy to understand. We can, however, apply the SIJR Model using any other personality inventory. Notice, we never gave anyone an actual test before we looked at personality. We can learn as much about a person's behavior by individual actions as we can from assessments. I say this because usually assessments are one dimensional, that is, the individual takes them alone. If, however, we administer a 360 assessment, whereby not only the individual but also people close to that person—subordinates, peers, boss, and others—rate the person, the data are more reliable. Some organizations use 360 assessments to help members understand each other's behaviors and to help leaders learn more about how others see them in comparison to how they see themselves. As Daniel Goleman points out, 360 assessments are excellent self-awareness tools and can enable leaders to learn how to improve their EI, emotional intelligence, as well as learn ways to get to their "ideal selves."[1] If you do not have access to these kinds of instruments, your best choice is to look at behaviors.

Embedded in each SIJR Conversation we found the Three C's. The first C is the orientation of change, namely, the person initiating the conversation does so knowing that change happens only if the other person is willing to make it happen. Even after a very good conversation that leads to resolving the problem, there is no guarantee the person's behavior will change. When we go into the conversation knowing that change depends on the other person, we are more realistic about the outcome.

The second C is compassion. No matter how contentious the conversation might be, if the speaker goes into that conversation with a sense of empathy, the chance for a positive outcome increases. The sticky situations we looked at demonstrated some instances where it was harder to feel compassion toward the other person than in other situations. Nonetheless, each time the speaker listened to the other person, invited that person to share, and attempted to understand the other person's point of view.

The third C is curiosity. In each SIJR Conversation, the speaker came from an orientation of curiosity. We wanted to learn what the other person was thinking. We were curious to understand their side of the issue. This sense of curiosity or a desire to learn more helped diminish defensiveness on both sides of the table. It did not eliminate defensiveness altogether, but defensive behaviors did not escalate it.

Finally, in applying the SIJR Conversation, we saw our speakers doing four things:

- **Specify the Problem.** Usually the problem was specified early in the conversation, but in some instances the speaker decided to wait. This decision often depended on the personality type of the other person. We also saw instances where the speaker had to respecify the problem later in the conversation or where speakers redefined the problem at the end of the discussion. In each sticky situation, however, the speaker identified the problem, which both parties finally resolved, when weighing the Decision Points.

- **Invite the Other Person to Talk.** Usually the speaker invited the other to talk immediately after specifying the problem. That approach set the tone for curiosity and interest in the other's point of view. Furthermore, in nearly every case, the speaker invited the other to participate in the resolution of the issue. Again, how much the speaker invited the other to talk depended on the other's personality. Some personalities talk more freely than others.

- **Join Feelings with Facts.** Expressing feelings about what was happening humanized the events. Depending on the speaker's personality, the ability to express feeling came with more or less ease. Nonetheless, in all our situations each speaker joined feeling with fact and in doing so tended to grab the other's attention and move toward problem resolution.

- **Resolve the Issue.** We never saw an SIJR Conversation that ended without resolution. The last case in Chapter 11 threatened to do so when Nichole requested time before making her decision to participate in the resolution. Her speaker conceded but insisted that she agree to stop the behavior. Had he simply agreed, the problem might have continued and/or escalated. Because each speaker invited the other to participate in the resolution, the final decision ended up being something both parties could live with.

This book demonstrated that the SIJR Model works in all kinds of office situations. We looked at sticky situations between bosses and subordinates, between vendors and customers or clients, and between co-workers. We also looked at situational situations, namely, in interviews, in meetings, as well as in romantic situations, in e-situations, and sticky etiquette situations. Although each of these cases involved different people with different personalities, we applied the model accordingly.

The SIJR Model works not only in an office environment but also in those thorny situations that affect our personal lives. Imagine the following sticky home situation.

STICKY SITUATION #26:
YOUR TEENAGE DAUGHTER IS BUSTED

Anita and Thomas Maxwell have a 17-year-old daughter, Katie, who enjoys popularity in school but whose grades hover at average. Katie has many friends of both sexes. Last weekend Katie asked her parents if she could go to her best friend's house for a party. Olivia, her best friend, lives in a neighborhood several blocks away. Anita and Thomas know the parents very well and felt comfortable granting Katie permission to go.

That Saturday night at midnight, the telephone rang. Thomas learned that his daughter and several other minors were at the police station having been arrested for underage drinking. Panicked, Thomas and Anita took off to the police station to rescue their daughter. They found her tearful, frightened, and unwilling to talk about the night's events. Following all the procedures with the police, Katie was released at 2 A.M.

The police informed the parents that the girls had gone to the house of an older boy whose parents were out of town for the weekend. The teens invited many other friends and eventually the noise level alerted the nearby neighbors, who called the police. Katie was one of six girls arrested.

APPLYING THE SAY IT JUST RIGHT MODEL

DECISION POINTS

The Maxwells weigh the costs. Anita and Thomas both feel betrayed, but they know their daughter was frightened by the events of the night before. Katie, who understands her parents' rules, had permission to go to Olivia's party, but not to go to someone else's house. The Maxwells further learned that there was not a party at Olivia's house that night after all. The girls had deliberately deceived both sets of parents. Nonetheless, the Maxwells feel fortunate that nothing serious happened to their daughter. She did not drive under the influence, and she was not injured in any way. They know, however, that if they do not face this incident, the next time could be more serious. According to the police, Katie will have to serve a six-month term of probation.

The Maxwells set limits. After a long discussion, Anita and Thomas decide that it would be best for Anita to talk with Katie. They further agree that they must punish Katie for what she did even though being at the police station and having to face her parents humiliated Katie and was something she will never forget. Furthermore, the term of probation for their daughter certainly frightened her. They, decide, however, that their number one desire is for Katie to be honest with them.

The Maxwells examine the power sources. Even though the Maxwells are the parents and as such they have a certain amount of power over their daughter, they recognize that Katie, too, has power. As a grown young woman, who is beginning to make her own decisions, she is free to go out with her friends. They cannot watch her every move, as they could when she was a toddler. If they simply impose their will without taking into account her needs, she may rebel.

PERSONALITY OVERLAY

Parents of teenagers, like the Maxwells, have a problem. Young people are not fully developed into their personalities. Furthermore, teenage traits tend to mask the kinds of behaviors we look at to determine someone's personality. For example, most teenagers have many friends. Would that make them Expressive? Most teenagers are impulsive and take risks. Does that mean they are Bold? Some teens obsess about their dress and their appearance. Does that make those teens Technicals? And, we all know how quick a teenage girl tends to cry, especially if she fears not getting what she wants. Does that make her a Sympathetic? The raging hormones make it difficult for the parents to determine the kind of personality they are dealing with. Most parents, however, know their children. They know what triggers a defensive or rebellious response.

One caution to all parents is to remember that your teenage child is not you. They are individuals with their own sets of personality characteristics. Simply because you think or feel a certain way does not mean your child thinks and feels that way. The best way to go into an SIJR Conversation with a teen requires a very open mind and the ability to adjust to surprises.

You, the parent, must also keep your emotions in check. You teenager will have enough emotions for the two of you. The SIJR Model will help you manage your emotions because it creates a sense of detachment.

SAY IT JUST RIGHT CONVERSATION

Anita told Katie she wanted to talk to her about what happened the night before. They decide to meet outside on the porch. Katie walks onto the porch with her head down as if awaiting the blows.

Anita walks over to her daughter and hugs her. "I'm so glad you are safe," she says. Katie doesn't say anything.

"Katie, I know how frightened you must have been last night. I could see the fear in your face when we came to the jail."

"Yeah," she says, still looking at the ground.

"Do you know how frightened your father and I were?"

She shakes her head.

"I know you think we make rules just to make your life miserable. But, what you don't understand is that we make those rules to protect you. We love you, and we don't want you to get hurt."

"I can take care of myself."

"Sure you can." Anita pauses. "Last night, though, showed us all that there are still times when it's nice to have parents, don't you think?"

Katie's shoulders drop.

Anita takes a deep breath. "I suppose what disappointed us more than anything was that you felt you couldn't be honest with us." **(Specifies the problem and joins feeling with fact.)** "Tell me what was going on there." **(Invites Katie to talk.)**

Katie shifts in her seat, her eyes flash. "You'd've never let me go to that party. Livie's parents wouldn't have let her either. So, well, you know. I guess we thought—we wanted to go so, we went."

"How do you feel about going now?"

"I wish I'd never met Jason. It was stupid."

"What was stupid?"

She puts a pillow on her lap and sighs. "You know. Going to the party in the first place. Jason wanted girls there. He kinda asked us to go. Livie knows him and his brother and another girl and they all wanted to go. So, we thought it would be fun. All of us and all. I didn't drink much, Mom. Just one beer."

"The problem is you don't have to drink much if you're too young to be drinking. You can get in a lot of trouble just being around alcohol. I'm sure the policeman told you that."

"He treated us like 4th graders. What a jerk."

"Katie, honey, last night you were 4th graders. It's hard to treat you like an adult when you don't think ahead."

"But we did think ahead. We were just gonna go for a couple of hours. But, well, when we got there, everybody wasn't there yet, and people wanted us to stay, and I met a cute guy. Livie wanted to stay, too, and, I guess, we just didn't look at the clock."

"That's all in the past. Why don't we focus on the future? What will you do next time Livie or anyone else wants you to deceive me and your dad?" **(Invites her to resolve the problem.)**

She takes a deep breath. "I shouldn't have done it. I guess all I was thinking was you wouldn't let me go. So, well, I just wouldn't tell you."

"Not telling is almost as bad as lying directly. It's called a sin of omission. Your dad and I were very disappointed that you felt you had to lie to us. We thought we had an open relationship with you." **(Joins feelings with fact.)**

"Yeah, so long as I do what you want." She turns away from her mother.

"Maybe we need to talk more about what it is you want. Maybe we haven't given you enough of a chance to share what you want." **(Looks for resolution.)**

Katie turns back and stares at Anita.

Anita asks, "I'm curious to know what might work for you the next time you want to do something you think we might disapprove of?"

She shrugs and grins. "Just let me go."

"What could you do that you didn't do this time?"

"Maybe I could've asked you first."

Her mother raises her brows. "But, you just said if you asked us, we'd have said no. What else could you do?"

"I could maybe tell you about what it is and why I want to go."

"If you had done that with this party, do you think we would have allowed you to go?"

She shakes her head. "Probably not."

"Why not?"

"I suppose because Jason's parents were out of town and, you know, because Jason's a university student and all."

Anita nods. "If we had talked about it and decided with you that this wasn't the best party for you to go to, what could we have done to make you feel better?"

There's a long silence. Anita waits and watches Katie.

"What if we gave you an option to do something else special? You could have had Livie and some of your other friends over or maybe we would've let you go to that Dave Matthews concert you want to go to."

"Awesome."

"Unfortunately we didn't have that conversation. I'm thinking that next time when you think we won't let you do something, why not ask? Even if you don't get to do that thing, we might allow you to do something else instead. How does that sound?"

"Aren't you going to punish me?"

"What do you think would be a fair punishment?"

She shrugs her shoulders. Anita waits through another long silence.

"Your dad and I talked. Last night scared you as much as it did us. You'll be on probation for six months. Those are punishments for having broken the law. But, no one has punished you for being dishonest with us. How about you consider a reasonable punishment for that and come back and tell us? I'd like to hear your ideas."

"Maybe if you ground me through next weekend. I wanted to go to see a new jazz band next Saturday. But . . . "

Anita frowns. "If we agree to the punishment you just named, what will you agree to do in the future?" (**Getting commitment to the resolution.**)

"I'll ask you when I want to do something with my friends and not lie."

"I'm glad to hear you say that. If you do that, you might be able to do more things than you think. But, if you deceive us again, we will have to consider much stiffer consequences."

ANALYSIS

Whether or not Katie changes her behavior is up to Katie. If she does lie to her parents again, she realizes that the consequences will be much harsher.

Anita showed a lot of compassion. She not only hugged her daughter at the beginning of the conversation, she also told her how worried and afraid she and her husband were. She recognized and acknowledged Katie's fear. This compassion eliminated some of the natural defensiveness she might have encountered.

Anita also displayed curiosity throughout the conversation. She wondered why Katie felt she had to lie. She wondered what she and her husband could do to make it easier for Katie to approach them. She wondered what punishment Katie thought was fair. All this curiosity brought Katie into the conversation.

Being a typical teen, Katie did not talk very much. Anita had to pull and tug and ended up suggesting the resolution. Nonetheless she gave Katie many opportunities to share her thoughts. Furthermore, she listened and didn't interrupt Katie during the conversation.

Specify the Problem. After Anita shared with her daughter how frightened she was and how frightened she knew her daughter was, she specified the problem. She did it in a gentle way by joining feeling with fact. "What disappointed us the most was that you felt you couldn't be honest with us." She used nonexplosive words, namely, "not honest" instead of "lied to us."

Invite the Other Person to Talk. Anita invited Katie to talk from the beginning. She asked her what happened. She showed curiosity with regard to what prevented Katie from telling them the truth. She invited Katie to help resolve the issue and to identify a fair punishment.

Join Feeling with Fact. This was a very emotional situation. Anita talked about her concern, her worry, her disappointment, her love. One reason Thomas agreed that Anita should talk to Katie was her ability to show her feelings. He feared his anger would further alienate his daughter. Parents are fortunate. It's best for both not to talk to the child together because that could feel intimidating. Instead parents can consider which of them might be the best suited to handle the SIJR Conversation. Anita kept her emotions in check. She did not yell or use accusatory language with her daughter. She may have cried during the conversation, particularly if Katie had cried. Her tears would show her daughter how hurt she was.

Resolve the Issue. Anita asked Katie what she might do next time. Anita's goal was for her daughter to be honest with them, even if she believes her parents won't allow her to do something. She prodded her daughter for solutions. Finally Katie said that next time she'd tell her parents what the event was and why she wanted to go. Anita also asked Katie what she thought would be a fair punishment for having distorted the truth. By getting Katie involved in her own punishment, Katie was more likely to follow through on what she agreed to do.

Conclusion

Parents of teens must stay alert and ready. Even after a successful SIJR Conversation, teens tend to surprise us. As a parent, your goal is to remain consistent and clear. The SIJR Model will enable you to think through the situations your teen presents, plan what you want to do within limits, communicate with compassion and curiosity, and reach a resolution.

You can model for your young, budding adult how to *say it just right*.

NOTE

1. Daniel Goleman, Richard Boyatzis, and Annie McKee, *Primal Leadership: Learning to Lead with Emotional Intelligence* (Boston: Harvard Business School Press, 2002), 133–34.

Appendix 1

Answers to Quizzes

YOUR STICKY SITUATION QUOTIENT

1. C
2. B
3. B
4. A
5. C
6. C
7. A
8. C

If you answered correctly on more than 6, you have a tendency to confront sticky situations head on. This tendency will enable you to experience more success with the SIJR Model.

CHAPTER 1

HOW STRAIGHT A TALKER ARE YOU?

1. False
2. False
3. False

4. True
5. False
6. False
7. True
8. False
9. False
10. False

If you answered correctly on 8 or more, you tend to be a straight talker. This skill will enable you to confront people when sticky situations arise. Question number 3 relates to being open when confronting someone. When you do not express your feelings, you tend to close up. This does not mean you should get overly emotional. If you are feeling emotional, you should postpone the SIJR Conversation until you feel calmer. Question 6 suggests immediately confronting someone with a "bad attitude." The answer is false because we do not know what a "bad attitude" looks like. You must first determine what the person does that makes you think he or she has a bad attitude. By so doing, you can address specific behaviors.

Chapter 3

Are You a Difficult Person?
Rate how difficult you are or you are not with the following scale: Add up your score:

- 8–20: Not too difficult (the lower the score the better)
- 12–31: Somewhat difficult
- 23–40: You are a difficult person

If you turn out to be somewhat difficult or a difficult person, you can change your behavior. Look at the questions where you had the highest scores. List three things you can do differently in order to lower those scores. It might be helpful for you to consider taking a 360 Leadership Assessment (see Appendix 2 for resources) and to hire a coach.

Chapter 7

How Good a Team Player Are You?

1. False
2. True
3. False
4. False
5. True
6. False
7. True
8. False
9. True
10. True

If you scored from 8–10, you are a great team player. That means you come to meetings on time or early, you voice your concerns even if everyone in the group disagrees, you work to bring in other opinions, and you recognize the value of team work.

Chapter 9

How Strategic an Interviewer Are You?

1. False
2. False
3. False
4. True
5. False
6. True
7. False
8. True
9. True
10. False

If you scored between 8–10, you are conducting strategic interviews. Strategic interviews focus on the person and are behavior based.

Strategic interviewers do not ask future related or hypothetical questions. A strategic interview uses the POINT process which includes planning, openness, intentional listening, and testing.

CHAPTER 10

RATE YOUR ETIQUETTE QUOTIENT

1. False
2. False
3. False
4. True
5. True
6. True
7. False
8. True
9. False
10. True
11. False
12. False

A score of 10 and above gives you a high Etiquette Quotient and tells you that you are aware of the changing workplace environment.

Appendix 2

Special Tools and Resources

Blogs

Say It Just Right™ Blog, www.totalcommunicationscoach.com/blog.
Water Cooler Wisdom, http://alexandralevit.typepad.com.
The Woman's Dish, http://womensdish.com.
The Big Bad Boss, www.bigbadboss.com.

360 Assessments—www.ccl.org

Even though there are many 360 assessments on the market, the Center for Creative Leadership is the gold standard. It provides the most reliable and valid data in comparison to a large data pool. It also provides online and paper administered instrumentation, scoring, and ratings at a fraction of the cost of other companies.

Benchmarks®—Designed to measure your leadership in comparison to other leaders at your level and in comparison to scores others give you. Measures 16 leadership capacities and 5 things that could potentially stall your career. Benchmarks is a great tool for mid-to-upper management and for people who show leadership potential. This instrument has the largest normative base.

360 By Design®—Designed to fit your organization or industry. Measures 11 competencies and 3 problems that can stall a career. Includes written comments by the raters. 360 by Design is a great tool for upper-level CEOs.

Executive Dimensions—Designed for CEOs, COOs, and presidents of noneducational organizations with more than 1,000 people. One hundred sixty-seven in the normative base. Measures 16 leadership capacities and includes written comments by raters.

Prospector®—Designed for high potentials, namely, people who demonstrate a talent and propensity for leadership. Also a great tool for identifying people with potential to work in another country and adapt to another culture. Measures 11 leadership capacities and includes written comments by raters.

INDIVIDUAL PERSONALITY INVENTORIES

My BEST Profile—BEST® instruments—This is the simplest instrument to administer and to understand. It provides basic information about personality traits. It scores 17 traits and actions in 16 situations. The instrument does not give a deep personality analysis. It simply provides enough information to enable others to better understand each other. James H. Brewer developed this instrument in 1988. For ordering information, check out www.hrdq.com.

DiSC Personality Inventory—This well-known assessment has a large data base. The Original DiSC Profile has been around for 35 years. For information check out www.discprofile.com.

Myers-Briggs Type Indicator®—This inventory is one of the most well known. It provides extensive information about personality type. The styles are difficult to remember and to define. If, however, you are looking at a deeper examination of your type, this is the best choice. For more information, check out www.myersbriggs.org.

OTHER BOOKS AND RESOURCES

For a listing of my favorite books and resources, check out this page on my Web site: www.totalcommunicationscoach.com/ongoing-learning.htm.

I constantly add books with my review of the contents. You will also find many new assessments to help you build your communication and leadership skills.

Index

About the Author

JOAN C. CURTIS, Ed.D., is a nationally known communications specialist who has conducted seminars and workshops in the public and private sector for more than 20 years. Her clients include major corporations as well as colleges and universities throughout North America. She is the author of *Strategic Interviewing: Skills for Savvy Executives* (2000). She has also written numerous articles that have been published in professional journals and on the Web, as well as in *Reader's Digest* and *Chicken Soup for the Working Woman's Soul.* Curtis received her doctorate in Adult Education from the University of Georgia.